Powerful S____ __ ____ng
Joy In Your Relationships

BRING OUT
THE
BEST
IN
OTHERS

Dr. Rick & Sheila Volweider

GET YOUR FREE GUIDED AUDIO MEDITATIONS AND MINDFULNESS GUIDE BOOK

Thank you for getting our book. We would like to give you a free copy of your updated *Quick Guide To Mindfulness*, which now contains four guided meditations, in both audio and transcript forms. We believe the guided meditations and the text will help you get more from *Bring Out The Best In Others*.

Download Your Free Guided Mindfulness Meditations and Book here: https://forms.aweber.com/form/99/2138863799.htm

DEDICATION

This book is dedicated to our mothers, Ruth Maurine Volweider and Loretta Elizabeth Farrell, who were the first to teach us how to bring out the best in others.

CONTENTS

ACKNOWLEDGMENTS

We extend our appreciation and gratitude to everyone who has been a part of our life's journey and without whom this book would not have written this book.

At the risk of leaving out a number of people, we want to acknowledge specific people. Connie Ragen Green helped us realize the first draft sounded too academic. Thanks to the Self Publishing School for helping us reach the finish line.

Mark Byrne offered an amazing 14-page critique and commentary on a later revision. Thanks to everyone, including John Brandeberry, Gala Valle, Janet Monahan, David Farrell and Charlie Farrell who read all or part of an earlier manuscript and provided comments.

Special thanks to Judy Henry for her comprehensive final edits, using her extensive grammar rainbow system.

Although in many cases, names and other identifying information have been changed, we appreciate those who agreed to have portions of their story described in our book.

Jeff Hatch-Miller provided excellent Neurolinguistic Programming (NLP) certification training we received in the 1980s. Both of us have used NLP ideas and strategies throughout our careers, and NLP informs several key assumptions and approaches in this book.

A major thanks to Eliot Cowan, whose talents, both as a teacher and healer, have impacted Rick and our family beyond words. You can learn more about Eliot in our chapter on Joy.

Although we would never have thought about writing this book if it were not for numerous people with whom our paths have crossed, we want to acknowledge two people very special to us. Jim Garner, who died in 2003, convinced Rick to join his counseling practice in 1986. Jim became both a friend and professional and personal mentor for Rick. Jackie Garner, Jim's partner for many years, has been a counselor, mentor and friend to both of us. Her enduring friendship, wise counsel and unfailing encouragement has had a lasting impact on both our immediate family and Sheila's extended family.

Finally, both of our daughters, Amy and Sara, gave us continued inspiration as well as adding to the book's content.

FOREWORD

During the fall of 2017, Rick Volweider and I walked along El Camino de Santiago in far northwest Spain for 17 days. During that enchanted journey, we had plenty of time to catch up on a multitude of subjects. Having stayed reasonably in touch since college days together at the University of Kansas, we were nonetheless amazed how much more we learned about each other. We caught up while hiking along this path so well-trodden by pilgrims for centuries. Between some truly awesome conversations of our own and so many of Rick's heartfelt dialogues with others from the world over along The Way, I knew that Rick was living his dream in real-time.

Bringing out the best in others truly is an internal mantra in Rick's life. There are many fortunate souls like me who are blessed with his calm, interested, non-judgmental and truly loving demeanor. Backed up by a career in private practice, Rick has treated the psychological needs of many. His special focus on children has been of particular note as Rick has experimented with and tested techniques over the years in lieu of pharmaceuticals where possible to address certain childhood and adolescent needs.

Sheila has been Rick's partner in life and spouse for decades. She from Ann Arbor, Michigan and he from Hutchinson, Kansas, they found each other in Phoenix, Arizona. Later, they raised their two daughters, Amy and Sara, on a farm in Kansas. Sheila brings extensive experience in social services and Rick a wealth of understanding through his clinical psychology practice.

Sheila has an uncanny way of immediately relating to people from all walks of life. With her warm smile, easy manner and genuine fascination with everyone she meets, Sheila, too, has an active internal mantra of bringing out the best in others. Together, Rick, the Ph.D. psychologist and Sheila, the super outgoing counselor, they make quite a team.

One could say through serendipity these two delightful souls met. Others might call it something beyond coincidence.

Jim Morley
Three Lakes, Wisconsin
July 1, 2018

Jim has enjoyed a life in service to others through the Peace Corps, the Organization of American States (OAS), World Neighbors, employee benefits consulting, non-profit boards participation and church roles.

PREFACE

After selling our home in Kansas, getting rid of 90 plus percent of our possessions, and passing on the unique aspects of Rick's psychology business, we began our odyssey in Central America on December 1, 2016. We roamed around Costa Rica and Panama for nearly four months, staying an average of five to seven days at each location. Residing at moderately to low-priced Airbnbs, hostels, and two hotels allowed us to get to know both locals and travelers engaged in their own adventures. Most of our fellow travelers were considerably younger than us and in their 20s to mid-30s.

While travelling, we increasingly noticed the friendliness, generosity, and kindness of everyone we met. Many encounters lasted seconds to minutes, but a substantial number evolved into hours and sometimes days of interaction. These longer lasting interactions often progressed into heartfelt conversations exploring weighty personal and sometimes philosophical concerns.

Many of our most delightful and meaningful moments with others resulted after something had "gone wrong." For instance, early in our adventures, we began the five-hour bus ride from San Jose to the port town of Puntarenas to catch a ferry to Paquera, and then a bus to Montezuma. Our bus seemed to travel an average of 10 miles an hour during the entire trip to Puntarenas, due to heavy traffic, road construction, and at least one accident.

After about seven hours, we arrived at Puntarenas to learn that the ferry had left, and the last one of the evening would be along in about four hours. It was already starting to get dark. Initially disappointed and upset by these developments, we found a reasonably priced restaurant with good food. We talked with several fellow passengers at the restaurant, including two beautiful young women who were traveling together. One had been traveling around the world the past year and had just met up with a friend for further adventures. We ended up delightfully spending the next five hours with them (including the ferry ride), sharing our lives and peculiarities. In retrospect, we were thankful for that extra-long bus ride and missed ferry.

Continuing our travels, we began to wonder why nearly all of our experiences with others were delightful and often meaningful, even when (or maybe especially when) exterior circumstances were not going as planned. In contrast, a number of our new friends did not share the same consistency of positive interactions with others, especially when things got tough.

Over some time, we began to see that our shared beliefs or assumptions about the world and other people, along with skills learned from both our professional and personal lives made all the difference in both our perceptions and outer realities of our adventures. Of course, acting in accordance with our beliefs and applying the skills we had learned was essential.

Considering what we had been doing, a single phrase came to mind. We were doing our best to *bring out the best in oth-*

ers. At some point, we realized that in doing so, we were also usually bringing out the best in ourselves.

Our adventure in Central America began less than a month after the 2016 US presidential elections. Although passionate disagreement between people in the country is not new, the hostility among those with opposing views appears to have reached new heights since the election.

We are concerned about the name calling and personal attacks on both sides of the political aisle in Congress in addition to their limited ability to work together. However, we are even more concerned with the discourse among average citizens. Readers' comments to political articles and videos posted on the internet, which too frequently resort to mutual condescension, disturb us. Some posts predict *civil war*. What we need now is *civil conversation* to deal with difficult and emotionally charged issues. We believe that a focus on bringing out the best in others is one way, maybe the best way, to do this.

Healing the cultural divide appears to be a monumental and nearly impossible endeavor. Working within larger systems, such as organizations, to effect change is both helpful and needed. However, we believe that all social change begins within and between individuals. In this book, you will learn to develop your connectedness with others by bringing out the best in yourself and them.

In both our professional and personal lives, we have seen occurrences of immediate or extended family members bringing out the worst in each other, which often brought suffering and alienation to all involved. As marriage partners, we have not been exempt from this, and it is still challenging to look back on times when our actions were clearly not bringing out the best in each other.

On the other hand, we have been blessed to experience (again both professionally and personally) an abundance of love, caring, and support from others. Without this support, you would likely not be reading this book.

———————————

This book is meant for anyone who is interested in increasing the quality of their relationships and connectedness with others. It contains the most effective beliefs, ways of thinking, and specific strategies we have learned for bringing out the best in others and ourselves.

Bringing out the best in ourselves and others is a journey that requires some shifts in our attitudes and beliefs, skill building in both our subjective mental processes and outward actions, and a commitment to live a life of bringing out the best with every chance we are given. The journey is solitary at times, as we look into our own beliefs, attitudes, and prejudices. But mostly the journey involves working, playing, and truly enjoying being with others in ways that increase our mutual sense of connectedness and cooperation.

This book is also for those wishing to participate in healing the increasingly treacherous, widespread, and deepening cultural divide toward which we have been moving.

You are invited to participate in the journey of bringing out the best by reading this book, contemplating the assumptions and ideas presented and trying out the strategies that seem most urgent and relevant to you. We also invite you to contribute actively by visiting our website at volweider.com.

Thank you,

Rick and Sheila Volweider
January 30, 2019

P.S. A few of the above paragraphs are taken directly from posts on our website, including "An Origin Story". For the complete article, go here: https://volweider.com/uncatego-rized/an-origin-story/

INTRODUCTION

Every interaction you have with another person, from passing someone on the sidewalk to discussing an important issue in an intimate relationship, presents an opportunity to impact their world and yours. With each interaction, you can choose to act in ways likely to brighten and add value to that person's day, strengthen your relationship, and increase your mutual well-being—in other words, *to bring out the best in others and yourself.* Or you can choose to act in a manner likely to dampen their mood, weaken the relationship, and decrease your mutual well-being. Of course, you can also decide to ignore that person, which may still have an impact on them (often negative) and your relationship.

You may be reading this book to help you connect and network better with others to accomplish your personal goals. You may be a supervisor who wants to increase productivity in your unit. You may want to deepen relationships in your family and help your spouse and children succeed in life. You may want to help others less fortunate than you. Or you may want to do all you can to promote cooperation and peace in your community, nation, and world.

All of these goals can best be achieved by learning and applying strategies to bring out the best in others. This book will get you started or refine your ability to bring out the best in people.

There are a number of books about how to cope with "difficult" people. This book will help you bring out the best in everyone you meet, including but certainly not limited to those difficult people. We will look at assumptions we make about ourselves, others, and our world, and how these beliefs influence our interactions with others, focusing on beliefs that help us bring out the best in others. There are different ways to see things, in a sense, different lenses you can put on to look at yourself, others, and the world. Next, we discuss some general practices to help prepare you to bring out the best in people. The final chapters cover specific techniques that can help you bring out the best in others.

This book was designed to be read in order, from beginning to end. However, feel free to skip around. You may want to start with the specific strategies in sections two and three. Some may use this book as a handbook, consulting the parts most relevant to their current concerns. Each chapter can stand alone and there are references to material in other chapters when clarification might be needed. However, we believe that understanding and working with the underlying assumptions, ways of thinking, and general strategies in earlier sections will help you apply the specific techniques in Section Three.

Section One asks you to consider *why* you would want to bring out the best in others and *where* and *with whom* you would want to do it. You are asked to consider what it means to bring out the best in others, what it might look like and how you would know when you are successful. We then give *our* view of what it means to bring out the best in others. Then we provide our take on the most helpful, practical, and prudent ways to think about bringing out the best in people.

Section Two provides general practices that give a foundation for the specific strategies discussed later. Chapter 3 focuses on learning to control impulsive responding to others, which is a necessity in bringing out the best in others. We cover meditation, mindfulness, ways to uncover unconscious beliefs and emotions, visualization strategies, and formal self-observation tools. Chapter 4 discusses how to increase empathy toward others, and Chapter 5 considers how to bring more joy into your life.

Section Three explores strategies to bring out the best in others. After briefly pointing out what not to do in Chapter 6, Chapters 7 through 10 look at developing the basic skills of open listening, communicating proactively, using expectations, and establishing rapport. Chapters 11 and 12 give other specific strategies.

The Conclusion adds closing remarks and looks ahead to what might happen if you made bringing out the best in yourself and others a focus in your life.

Hopefully, you will make this book an interactive experience. We invite you to pause and think when we ask a question. Even better, write down your responses. Your answers to various questions may change over time and as you read this book. Writing things down helps preserve what you were thinking at the time and makes it easier to compare with your current thinking. You literally see your thoughts, feelings, and beliefs differently when you write them down, instead of just letting them flutter around in your mind. Also, it is easier to build upon what you give external expression by recording your interaction with this book in some form (handwriting, typing, voice recording). We believe this will significantly add to the value of reading this book.

You are invited to participate in our Bring Out The Best Community at http://volweider.com/. We will be adding blog posts related to bringing out the best, and your contributions are welcomed.

When you focus on bringing out the best in everyone you meet, you bring out the best in yourself. You have probably heard the story of the elder explaining that two wolves live inside all of us—the constructive/good one and the destructive/bad one. Each of us determines which one grows by deciding which one we will feed (the most). You can choose which wolf you feed in others as well as the wolf you feed in yourself.

We recently listened to a 2017 TED talk by Pope Francis. In this talk, he eloquently states much of the heart of this book's message. He stresses the bonds we share with others and the importance of meeting people where they are. You can listen to it here: https://www.ted.com/talks/pope_francis_why_the_only_future_worth_building_includes_everyone/transcript#t-50337

SECTION

ONE

MINDSET

We use the word *mindset* rather broadly, to refer to our ways of thinking about various things—the attitudes, beliefs, and underlying assumptions we make. Exploring one's attitudes, beliefs, and assumptions about a topic is crucial before diving into the specifics.

Chapter 1 discusses the Why, Whom, What, Where, and When of bringing out the best in people. You are asked to consider your own thinking and feelings about these questions. Our beliefs about what it means to bring out the best in ourselves and others is then presented.

Chapter 2 covers specific beliefs or assumptions about people and life that can enhance our abilities to bring out the best in ourselves and others.

We believe that however you answer the basic Why, Whom, What, Where, and When questions in Chapter 1, you will get value from the book if you read it, think about it, and apply at least some of the preparatory practices and specific strategies described in Sections Two and Three. The value you get out of this book will likely be directly related to how much time and effort you expend in both understanding and doing these practices and strategies.

Accepting, or at least temporarily suspending your disbelief concerning Chapter 2 assumptions, is a necessary component of bringing out the best in yourself and others. For instance, if you don't believe there is a basic goodness in most people, trying to bring out their best would likely seem futile. Why try if there is nothing good to help bring out?

At this point, you may be asking, "What if I don't agree at all with your basic assumptions? Should I stop reading here?" Let's take a few moments to explore this further.

Carol Dweck has studied a particular form of mindsets for much of her career. She distinguishes between fixed and growth mindsets. In her own words:

> In a fixed mindset students believe their basic abilities, their intelligence, their talents, are just fixed traits. They have a certain amount, and that's that. ... In a growth mindset students understand that their talents and abilities can be developed through effort, good teaching and persistence. They don't necessarily think everyones the same or anyone can be Einstein, but they believe everyone can get smarter if they work at it.[1]

Dweck found that students with a growth mindset are more likely to continue working diligently in the face of obstacles and difficulties, compared to the fixed mindset students.

Although Dweck has primarily focused on fixed and growth mindsets concerning basic abilities, talents, and intelligence, our thinking extends this to other aspects of being human. Specifically, we believe some people have a relatively fixed mindset concerning their beliefs and assumptions about themselves, others, and the world; while others have a growth mindset about these beliefs and assumptions. Persons with a growth mindset think their beliefs and assumptions are open to change, given the right conditions. This may involve sensory experience, facts learned from reliable sources, logical arguments in addition to self-observation, inquiry, and intuition.

Rick used to believe that he would be swarmed by mosquitos and other flying insects if he came to Central America—especially along their beaches and rainforests. After our first four months in Costa Rica and Panama, mostly in coastal and rainforest areas, I had not seen a single mosquito and had not been bitten by one. I seem to have had a growth mindset, at least on this topic, since I have come to believe my actual sensory experience more than my prior assumptions.

So if you are at first skeptical about our assumptions in Chapter 2, test them out. The simplest way to do this is to temporarily make believe that you agree with them, try out the practices and strategies, and see what happens—and then trust in your own sensory feedback and intuition. It's a bit like that old and worn saying, "Fake it till you make it." Also as you will read in Chapter 2, we are not trying to convince you that these beliefs and assumptions fully represent eternal truth (although they might). However, we are confident that making these assumptions while skillfully applying the specific strategies, will significantly increase your ability to bring out the best in others.

1

BRINGING OUT THE BEST IN OTHERS: WHY, WHO, WHAT AND WHERE

Why bring out the best in people?

Why would you want to bring out the best in people? We assume that most of you have some thoughts about this or you would not have started reading. Before reading further, please stop and think a bit about this question. Please take some time to think about your reasons and maybe what other people's reasons might be. We encourage you to write these down or record them in some other manner.

When Rick was in fourth grade, a teacher asked him why he had done something. I don't recall what I had done, but I suspect the teacher wasn't so happy about it. As I now remember, I thought for a while and then told her at least seven reasons I had done it. I think she may have disliked my answers more than whatever I did in the first place. There are often numerous, if not countless, reasons we do things or are attracted to some things and not others.

Please think about this question again, just a little longer. Why do you want to bring out the best in people? What are your reasons? When you think about your reasons for bringing out the best in others, we invite you to interpret the word "reasons" broadly. Its meanings might include: cause, basis, rationale, motive, motivation, purpose, point, aim, intention, intent, objective, goal, explanation, justification, defense, pretext, and so on.

————————————

Okay, hopefully you have given this question some thought. The following are some possible reasons for wanting to bring out the best in others. Consider them and note any that you resonate with.

- I want people to treat me better.
- I want people to listen to me more.
- I want people to help me more.
- I want to get more of what I want.
- I want to be happier.
- I want to feel I've accomplished something meaningful in my life.
- I want to enjoy being with others.
- I want to help others.
- Our family/community needs to learn to bring out the

best in each other to more fully support one another.

- Our family/community needs to learn to bring out the best in each other to constructively build a more robust and secure future.
- Our family/community needs to learn to bring out the best in each other to resist forces that oppose our values and beliefs.
- Our family/community needs to learn to bring out the best in each other so we can join together for social change which represents our beliefs and values.
- I want to be of service to others.
- I know others have a lot to teach me and I want to learn from them.
- We all have a lot to learn from each other, and I'd like to help create a situation where that occurs.
- I want to cooperate with everyone in the most constructive way and in a way that benefits both (or all) of us.
- I want more peace and happiness for all of us.
- I want to foster peace and cooperation with everyone I meet.
- This world may only survive if many of us focus on bringing out the best in everyone we meet.
- I want to contribute to making the world a better place.
- I'd agree to anything if we can just move on with it.

With which of these reasons did you identify? What do you think are the best reasons for trying to bring out the best in people? Our view is that all these reasons are valid on their own terms. Some reasons represent levels of development that are more inclusive and lead toward increased connectedness with others.

Who are the people with whom you want to bring out the best?

This is a related question, and we have inferred some possible answers above. A slightly different way to put the question: When you think about bringing out the best in people, who comes to mind? You might think of specific individuals or groups of people. Is it mostly people you already know well, know a bit, or don't know at all right now? Are you thinking more about people at work, family, or friends? Why did those people come to mind and not others?

You might find that as you thoughtfully read this book, your answers to these questions changes or expands.

Unless some extraterrestrial explorers are residing on Earth and have picked up a copy of this book, we assume everyone reading this is human. As humans, most of us have not developed the capacity to deal healthily with everyone who crosses our path. Our section on shadow work in Chapter 3 touches on ways to grow in this area. However, you will likely encounter some people for who you are not ready. And sometimes you are thrust into spending some time with them due to family, work, or social obligations. You might need to interact with them as superficially as possible and might decide you will not talk with them about controversial topics. You might choose to unfriend them on Facebook. You might ignore them completely. Or as one wise person recently told us, "You might need to find a way to at least not bring out their worst."

Of course, the other group of people you should strongly consider not interacting with are those whom you believe are physically dangerous to you. Hopefully, your assessment of their dangerousness will not solely rely on stereotypic assumptions concerning race, religious orientation, gender, etc.

What is the best in people that you are trying to bring out?

Before we discuss our viewpoint on this question, please think about (and ideally write down) what you believe. Other ways to put the question are: How would you know that you are bringing out the best in others? What would it look like? What kinds of behaviors would they be exhibiting?

———————————

We think that most of us can agree that the following list of behaviors and inner qualities constitutes the *good,* if not the *best,* in people. Here is our list followed by a discussion of each quality.

- Honesty
- Trust in themselves and others
- Openness in communication with others—the ability to dialogue with others instead of soliloquizing, debating or lecturing
- Ability to explore things in depth, instead of just superficially
- A sense of playfulness, fun, joy, and laughter
- Compassion toward others and themselves
- Intent and ability to cooperate with others

Honesty

Most of us define honesty as being truthful and generally believe it is a desirable quality. However, there are several ways to look at truth and honesty. The most common meaning of *honesty* is being truthful about external happenings—what has occurred or is present in the physical world. Asking your three-year-old if she wrote on the kitchen wall with a crayon is an inquiry into this type of truth and honesty. Let's say you saw her do it and she says she did not do it although she is holding the same color of crayon that is on the wall. She is being dishonest or untruthful about her artistic endeavors.

The other major type of honesty deals with the outward expression of inner truth. Integrity can be defined as the quality of being honest and consistently acting in accord with one's principles. This type of honesty involves being true to yourself. Following your deep convictions and principles as well as recognizing your "true" feelings are examples of this type of honesty and integrity. Becoming aware of and integrating our feelings, thoughts, and beliefs is an ongoing process that we develop throughout our lives. Recognizing and incorporating our unconscious thoughts and emotions (including our *shadow),* discussed in Chapter 3, is a lifelong pursuit for most of us.

Sometimes there is internal conflict about how to be honest and act with integrity. An example: Aunt Sally gives you another fruit cake for Christmas (you already have 17 of them in the basement freezer—a lot but not enough to build a bomb shelter), and you say, "Thank you, I love your fruitcakes." There is an incongruity in what you think/feel about the fruit-cake and what you say to Aunt Sally. At this point, one might judge that you are being dishonest or showing a lack of integrity. However, let's say that among your most basic values is the directive not to hurt others unnecessarily. Letting on that you view her gift as useful only for self-defense would likely hurt her feelings. So being honest about your fruitcake feelings would betray one of your deep values concerning how to treat others. Note that this type of dishonesty (often referred to as white lies) is often taught to children in Western societies. These children are often confused by this because nobody has explained the issue to them, or they have not progressed beyond their black and white thinking.

There is another subtle form of dishonesty which Rick often saw in his clinical practice with families. Back to the three-year-old artist. Remember that mom has seen her daughter color the kitchen wall before she asks her, "Did you color the wall?" Usually, in our culture, we ask questions because we want to know the answer. It is taken for granted we don't already know the answer, or we would not be asking. Of course in the above case, the mother already knows the answer. Her real question is "Will you (her child) tell me the truth about it?" At the least, this mother is being disingenuous in asking the question.

Determining a person's honesty can get a little complicated. A lesson here is not to be so quick to judge others' honesty and other characteristics or behaviors you see in them.

Trust in themselves and others:

Can we all agree that *trust* often leads to love, peace-of-mind, and comfort; while *distrust* often leads to fear, anger, anxiety, and misery? Furthermore, these qualities have a reciprocal nature. For example, as you feel more trusting with someone, you may feel more affection toward the person and as you feel more affection toward them, you start to trust them more.

Openness in communication with others, with the ability to dialogue with others instead of only soliloquizing, debating or lecturing

When you feel trusting toward another, it is a lot easier to be more open and honest about what you feel and think. As pointed out several times in this book; ideally, open communication goes both ways. One can listen to others, not prejudging and evaluating everything they say while formulating one's rebuttal, but instead, listening with openness and curiosity to better understand their opinions and points of view. We can also be open in how we *talk* with others by being as open and honest as is appropriate and reasonable for the current situation. Chapter 7 explores open listening in detail.

Ability to explore things in depth, instead of just superficially

You can probably sense when a person is speaking at a superficial level and when they are digging deeper into their beliefs, thoughts, and feelings. You can also likely recognize those times when you are in a dialogue with another person that is free-flowing and non-defensive, where you both feel delighted in getting to know and understand the other in new and fascinating ways. We believe these are times when you two are bringing out the best in each other.

A sense of playfulness, fun, joy, and laughter

We believe that joy is an inherent part of our being which often has been pounded down by our frenetic pace and over-stimulation. Helping yourself and others recapture some of that joy and laughter is bound to assist in bringing out your and others' best. Please see Chapter 5 on Cultivating Joy.

Compassion toward others and themselves

Empathy is the sense of understanding the feelings and worldviews of others while *compassion* includes a concern and desire to alleviate the suffering of others. *Compassionate action* is actually doing something, taking action on that concern and wish to help others. We believe that a significant demonstration of bringing out one's best is acting compassionately toward others. Chapter 4 explores these issues in detail.

Intent and ability to cooperate with others

A critical element of a functional society is the desire and ability for people to *cooperate* with each other. Even hunter-gatherer tribes needed cooperation among their members to hunt, kill, and process large animals as well to gather and preserve plant-based food. Every cell in our body has to cooperate with our other human and non-human cells, including bacteria and viruses, for our bodies to regain and maintain our health. When you are cooperating with others in a constructive or enjoyable activity, you are likely bringing out the best in yourself and others.

To revisit the question of how we know when we are bringing out the best in others, please consider this question at its most basic level: *When you are engaged in a one-to-one relationship, how do you know, moment to moment, that you are bringing out the best in each other?* Again, please think about this before moving on.

Our answers take the form of two main questions.

- Did I enjoy being with the person and felt they also enjoyed our time together while feeling a bit closer to each other in some way?

- Did I feel we accomplished something that was constructive? This could take the form of learning something new, understanding something in a new light, experiencing improved communication, physically producing something, or …

Before moving on to the next question, note that there are other ways of thinking about what it means to bring out the best in others. The gardener analogy detailed in the introduction to Section Three points to this perspective for bringing out the best in others.

Where and when should you bring out the best in others?

The quick answer is everywhere and all the time. However, there is a bit more to say about this. We realize that we all get tired and just want to relax sometimes. Even the most gregarious person needs some alone time. You may be deep in your thoughts at times while you are walking down the sidewalk and don't want to acknowledge or relate to others right then. Of course, that's okay; everyone needs some downtime. But generally, we encourage you to look at any encounter with others as an opportunity to bring out the best in them and yourself. Just acknowledging another person by looking at them and smiling can have an impact.

Another exception to keep in mind is your own and others' safety. There are areas and times in almost every city and some rural areas where it might not be safe to walk and greet everyone in your path. You may see some people, even in relatively safe situations, that you decide to avoid, at least at that time. Use your judgment where safety and well-being might be an issue.

2

BASIC ASSUMPTIONS

We all have basics beliefs or assumptions about the world and how it operates. Often these beliefs are so fundamental to our being that we don't notice them. It's a bit like fish not being aware they are in water since water is a constant in their lives.

Since the primary purpose of this book is to help you bring out the best in others, you may be wondering what beliefs and assumptions have to do with it. First, how we think about and emotionally perceive others is strongly influenced by our general beliefs and assumptions about people and the world. And the way you think and feel about others significantly affects how you behave toward them. Some beliefs enhance our ability to bring out the best in others while other beliefs diminish this ability.

Second, it can be helpful to understand that other people have different beliefs and assumptions about the world than you do, and this largely accounts for why they may do things very differently than you would.

Rick became more appreciative of the role of beliefs in our lives, partly as a reaction to the limited views of psychology and psychotherapy at the first graduate school he attended in the 1970s. The psychology department viewed behaviorism as the only legitimate source of knowledge to guide therapeutic practice. Behaviorism focuses only on observable behaviors and dismisses mental activities including thoughts and beliefs. I began searching for alternative viewpoints. I discovered Albert Ellis's Rational Emotive Behavior Therapy and Aaron Beck's Cognitive Therapy, both of which emphasized the effects of our thoughts and beliefs on our emotions and behavior.

Sheila and I met in the mid-1980s. She was skilled in hypnosis, and together we trained for certification in neurolinguistic programming (NLP). NLP uses our inner thoughts, beliefs, feelings, and perceptions together with our behavior to create change in ourselves and others. Through our various training, and more importantly from our 30-plus years of practice and self-reflection, we have come to see beliefs as a foundation that influences our perception and interpretation of every experience as well a significant influence of what we do.

Below are some primary assumptions that impact how we think about and treat others. Although this chapter provides some scientific support for these assumptions, we know these beliefs have served us well in bringing out the best in others as well as providing healthy and constructive ways to think about life in general.

The following assumptions are discussed.

- People are basically good and doing the best they can.

- Everything you experience contains a lesson to be learned.
- Everything you do potentially makes a difference but maybe not when and how you want it to do so.
- All people want to be happy and not suffer.
- People have different perspectives and about things, which may or may not match yours.

People are basically good and doing the best they can

When using the phrase *bringing out the best in people*, we are presuming people have good inside of them that we might assist in bringing out. You don't have to put the *good* inside of them. It's already there. Many wisdom traditions support this idea—that all people have inborn goodness inside of them.

Science is beginning to catch up to these wisdom traditions. Warneken and Tomasello have done studies on helping behaviors with children 14 to 18-months-old.[2] The experiments involved different situations where an adult, whom the child did not know, was having trouble completing a task. In one condition, the adult was hanging towels on a clothesline, "accidentally" dropped a clothespin on the floor, and was unsuccessful in reaching for it. In another situation, the adult was putting away magazines in a cabinet but could not open the doors because his hands were full. The results showed that kids slightly over one-year-old often spontaneously helped others. Their further studies found that children who got a material reward after helping were less likely to continue to help compared to children that did not get rewarded. These findings add to the evidence that toddlers' helping behavior does not come from social or material reinforcement but is more likely an inborn quality.

Researchers Paul Bloom and Karen Wynn at Yale's Infant Cognition Center have found that 3-month-old babies show a preference to a puppet who *helps* another puppet open a box compared to a puppet who *interferes*. This finding hints that these judgments have very early developmental origins.

A close cousin to the above belief is that people are doing the best they can with the resources available to them at the moment, a motto we learned in NLP training.

Rick worked with kids who had ADHD, oppositional behaviors, and school difficulties for about 25 years. During the first five years of working with oppositional children and teens, I accepted the mainstream belief that these kids could do better *if they really wanted to* and my job was to *motivate* them to do better with the help of their parents and school. Following the leaders in the field at that time, I taught every parent highly structured behavioral programs, involving rewards for good behavior and non-physical punishment for bad behavior. After several years, I finally realized this approach was not working well with most of the kids I saw.

After several more years of trying to refine behavioral approaches, I came to see, partly through Ross Greene's writings and seminars, that the underlying belief that these kids just needed stronger motivation was flawed or at least seriously limited. Ross Greene's conviction, *Kids will do well if they can,* led to more cooperative approaches that brought on more desirable and longer lasting changes. In this view, problematic behavior occurs because the person does not have the skills or abilities needed to deal appropriately with the present circumstances. It's usually not because they just *want* to be *bad*. Inside they want to be good and do well; however, they don't know how to respond to the current situation in better ways.

Although about 75 percent of my practice focused on children and teens, parents or other caregivers participated in part or all of most sessions. I extended this belief to everyone in the room—that they were doing the best they could with the skills and mindset they currently had. Sheila also made these assumptions concerning the chronically mentally ill adults with whom she worked. In short, these assumptions apply to all of us, at any age.

Some may think our perspective is Pollyannaish or excessively optimistic concerning this assumption. However, assuming that we all have goodness does not imply that we cannot act badly.

Remember the story mentioned in the Introduction about the elder explaining to his grandson that two wolves live inside us all? According to most internet sources, the story originated from the Cherokee Indians, was transmitted word-of-mouth for a long time, and now has various written versions. As one version of the story goes...A boy is talking to his grandfather about some injustice another boy did to him. The grandfather tells the boy that two wolves live inside him. One wolf is bad, evil, hateful, and spiteful toward others while the other wolf is good, loving, compassionate, and forgiving. The two wolves are constantly fighting for control inside the grandfather. The boy asks, "Which wolf wins?" Grandfather replies, "The one I feed."

Most spiritual/wisdom traditions address good and evil, often with stories. Science is learning more about how our brains give us the capacity to act selfishly and egotistically but also communally for the benefit of others. We often judge different aspects of ourselves and others as being good or bad.

Our point here is that we do have a choice of what we focus on. Perhaps the law of attraction should be called the law of attention. What is attended to will generally grow and become more abundant in our lives while what is ignored typically shrinks and becomes scarcer. Of course, there are limits here. However, by attending to the good we see in people and interacting with them with the intention of bringing out their best, good things will probably follow.

Everything you experience contains a lesson to be learned

We've all heard a version of these following statements: *That which doesn't kill you strengthens you. God never gives you anything you can't handle.* We believe that any experience you've made it through teaches you something and thus makes you more capable of coping with whatever happens next if you are willing to learn from it.

Similarly, the Buddhist concept of *beginner's mind* invites us always to be open to learning new things from every experience.

In a talk at the 2017 Influence and Impact Summit, Ray Edwards expressed his belief that everything about our lives is here to help us become who we were meant to be and to learn who we really are. This thinking encourages us to learn from every experience and view every human interaction as a chance to learn from, teach, receive from, or give to others.

One way this applies to bringing out the best in others is to view all encounters with others, even those that are difficult, as learning experiences for all involved.

Everything you do potentially makes a difference but maybe not when and how you want it to do so

You may not see the results of your attempts to *bring out the best in people* immediately but realize it may have an impact at some point in their lives. Sheila counseled teenage girls at a residential placement in Texas in her early thirties. I especially remember three girls with whom I worked for months; one of them addressed me as Mom. After coming in on a Monday morning, I learned that the three had run away together during the weekend. I was devastated by feelings of loss, sadness, and discouragement. I had poured so much of myself into these three girls and for what?

While visiting my mom the next weekend, I happened to see a TV show where the host was interviewing a young man who had been in multiple placements, including juvenile detention, residential programs, and foster care homes. The interviewer asked what helped him become a happy, successful adult. He replied that a woman conducting one of his many placement interviews told him something that made him realize he had value. He could not remember what she had said, but he remembered how he felt when she said it—a kernel of worth and a glimmer of hope. Although changes were not immediate, he believed this kernel started germinating over a period of years. As the seed grew, he was able to make more positive decisions about his actions and life.

This show had a massive impact on me. I began to understand that every effort to reach out, care, acknowledge, and love can make a difference, often without our awareness. The young man on TV that day did not know how he had changed my life.

I realized it was up to those teenagers to put our caring and counsel into action on their own timetable, not ours.

I later ran into a young woman with whom I had previously worked. She had shown little progress while I had worked with her. She told me that she had heard everything that the other staff and I said to her, but she could not put any of it into action at the time. Resisting authority was her prime directive back then. However, when the time was right for her, she found herself making choices consistent with what she had learned from us.

The main thing I learned from these experiences was that the world often does not operate on my time frame. I was able to release this expectation to a large degree. I concluded that everything you do potentially makes a difference but maybe not when you want it to do so or in the specific form you had imagined it.

All people want to be happy and not suffer

One of the assumptions that is central to the authors of *The Book Of Joy* is that *all of us want to be happy and avoid suffering*. This assumption can be a backbone for developing empathy for others because most of us can buy into the idea that since we want to be happy and not suffer, it's likely others feel the same. However, remember that what brings happiness for one person may bring indifference or even sadness for another. If you want to bring out the best in a person, you first have to understand who that person is, what they want, what brings them joy, and so on.

Chapter 5 on cultivating joy explores these issues further.

People have different perspectives about things which may or may not match yours

Have you ever thought, "The world would be a lot better if everyone believed and thought like me. I must be believing and seeing the world in the right and best ways, or I'd be thinking differently. I don't know what's wrong with you if you don't agree with me."? Join the club!

People have different beliefs and different ways of seeing the world, and our worldviews don't always match theirs. You don't need to change your perspectives and beliefs to connect with others, but you do need to suspend your judgment while exploring others' views. Chapter 7 goes into detail about how to do this.

SECTION

TWO

PREPARING YOUR BRAIN AND MIND

L ouis Pasteur is often quoted as saying, "Luck (or fortune) favors the prepared mind." Getting our minds and brains in shape helps us to more skillfully apply specific strategies for bringing out the best in others. This is much like getting our bodies in shape boosts our performance in any sport. Engaging in the practices discussed in this section is helpful before applying the strategies in Section Three. However, consistently applying these practices is needed to keep your mind and brain in the best shape, much like elite sports stars continue basic training exercises.

Controlling our impulsive reactions to what others do and say is a prerequisite in bringing out their best. Rick vividly remembers a therapy session with Bob, a high school senior, and his parents. Bob was telling us a long list of things he wanted to do following graduation. At one point, his mother interrupted him, saying in a loud and exasperated tone, "That's the dumbest thing I've ever heard." Bob didn't say much more during the rest of that session.

Chapter 3 covers meditation, uncovering your shadow, enhancing self-observation, mental rehearsal, stealing behavior, and buying yourself time to cool down. These practices help you bring out the best in yourself and others in all sorts of ways. They are included in Chapter 3 because they can significantly help you control impulsive responding—lengthening the space between what happens and your response to it.

Developing empathy toward others, covered in Chapter 4, is needed to apply Section Three strategies from your heart, instead of mechanically and robotically. We believe others can immediately tell the difference.

Chapter 5 explores one of the most important ways to bring out the best in people—cultivating your own joy of life.

As you do this, you will naturally find or be guided into ways of helping bring out the best in others.

To add a little balance to the heady stuff in this section, note that according to Wikiquote, Louis Pasteur also said, "A bottle of wine contains more philosophy than all the books in the world."

3

LENGTHENING THE SPACE BETWEEN WHAT HAPPENS AND YOUR RESPONSE

During our combined 50-plus-years of training and experience in counseling, we have pretty much mastered the ability to listen carefully before responding and to avoid knee-jerk reactions, at least during client sessions. However, when it comes to personal communication, especially with each other, we are still works in progress.

About 10 years ago, we started using the phrase, *defending our position,* to describe a lot of our non-helpful verbal communication with each other. Both of us struggled not to quickly interrupt the moment we felt the other person was challenging our position on the matter. Although *realizing* we were defending our own views at the expense of not listening to the other person's viewpoint did not make us stop doing it.

And the result was that we were mostly talking to ourselves instead of each other.

When operating on knee-jerk time, things seem to happen in a flash; the mind is barely conscious of the process and its response. We usually realize what we have said and its negative impact sometime after it leaves our mouths.

Several things have been helpful for us in breaking (or at least weakening) this habit.

- Acknowledging and identifying what we were doing as *defending our position*
- Talking about this issue when calmer instead of at the heat of the moment
- Expressing our mutual feeling that this way of *defending our positions* was not helpful in solving problems or enhancing our relationship
- Stating to each other our intention to do our best to stop or at least cut down on this behavior
- Learning to say, "Can we talk about this later?"

The importance of physiology

Lengthening the time/space between what happens in the exterior world and one's outer reaction or response to it is part of growing up. Given this extra time, one can observe and reflect on their thoughts and feelings while considering responses that are most likely to bring out the best in themselves and others.

Let's look at how these knee-jerk reactions happen. Cognitive-behavioral therapy and pop psychology tell us that events do not directly produce our emotions. What someone just said does not directly make you feel a certain way. Instead, our interpretation of the situation as expressed by our self-talk and imagination brings forth our emotional response, which we then act on.

Although this may be a fruitful way of thinking about our mental, emotional, and verbal responses, it is also crucial to recognize that our immediate reactions to many things are physiological. When we end up feeling upset or angry about what someone has said, our body is usually the first to respond to the person's comments. This includes physiological changes such as variations in blood pressure, heart rate, electrical brain activity, sweat gland production, muscle tension, and a lot more.

In 2007, Rick was diagnosed with stage 4 head and neck cancer. The cancer started in the tongue and spread to the lymph nodes in the neck. Sheila and I sat in a small room in an old, eerie building at the University of Kansas Medical Center. I got the special seating in what appeared to be a dental chair across from Sheila and the physician. Sheila had prepared a list of about 20 questions for the doctor, who specialized in this type of cancer. He went through the questions with brief and straight-forward answers. The five-year survival rate with treatment wasn't so good, but they pronounced you cured if they found no remaining cancer after five years. And yes, they might have to cut out my tongue, but you can still speak with an electronic device.

My mind was swimming with thoughts and emotions. When it was finally over, and I got out of the chair, I noticed a sizable amount of water on the floor below me. Although I wouldn't have been surprised if I had wet my pants, the water was due to profuse sweating. The psychologist part of me found it fascinating that hearing specific words could unleash a flood of perspiration. The rest of me was scared to death.

We believe the most accurate and helpful way of thinking is that our physiology, thoughts and beliefs, and emotions are influencing each other and our responses, all the time. One could imagine that as I heard the doctor's words, my physiology moved into stress response mode, which heightened my fear and dire self-talk, which increased the physiological stress response, which further increased fear and dire self-talk and on and on.

Let's now explore specific practices and strategies to help you eliminate or at least slow down your knee-jerk reactions.

Meditation and mindfulness

Meditation and mindfulness practice helps develop an inner calmness and even temper, especially important in difficult and trying situations. One way it does this is by keeping our physiological processes within a narrow range. In other words, it helps keep the heart rate, blood pressure, adrenaline output, etc., more constant. If practiced regularly for a relatively long period of time, this can significantly help lengthen the space between what happens and your response.

Mindfulness is the practice of focusing one's awareness on the present moment while acknowledging and accepting one's feelings, thoughts, and bodily sensations without judgment.

A simple mindfulness practice is to sit and focus on your breathing. Sit comfortably, shut your eyes, or with eyes slightly open, focus about three feet away. Feel and hear the air as you breathe in and out through your nose. Breathe from deep in your lungs using your diaphragm muscle, which is below your rib cage, not your chest muscles. At some point, you will likely get so absorbed by your thinking or imagination that you will forget about your breathing. When you remember, just return your focus to your breath. You might start with five minutes and gradually increase to 20-minute daily sessions. We'd recommend practicing daily but even two or three times per week would be a good start.

Many people find that silently repeating some word or phrase is helpful. One technique is to repeat the word "one" with each exhalation. Another strategy is to count each inhalation and exhalation, starting with *one* during the first inhalation, *two* while exhaling, *three* during the second inhalation and so on, up to *ten*. Then start counting from "one" again. You will probably find you have stopped counting at some point. Start counting again. You can also repeat a mantra or a phrase that has religious/spiritual significance for you. Do not give yourself a hard time for not doing things perfectly. That's why they call it a *practice*. Even advanced and esteemed yogis keep practicing.

As you advance in your mindfulness or meditation practice, you might find it helpful just to sit, doing nothing in particular. Observe whatever is happening in your interior and exterior worlds without trying to change it. When a thought, image, or feeling occurs, "watch" it come and go. Make no effort to hold on to it, judge it, or push it aside. Become the observer.

We also enjoy walking meditation. Walk slowly while focusing on each step. Feel your contact with the Earth during every step. Breathe slowly, deeply, and comfortably. You can use one of the mental strategies given above but please keep your eyes open.

As you develop in your practice, you will probably find it

easier to sustain a calm and observant manner in other areas of your life. When you wash dishes, focus your attention on this task. When you realize your mind has been pulled away by concerns of the past or future, return your attention to the dishes. Being fully present while doing a task is similar to what people report during peak performance.

For many, it may be best to join a meditation, mindfulness, or prayer group led by an experienced teacher and practice together. However, there are many excellent books on meditation practice to get you started. There are also many apps you can download to assist in your meditation practice. We think *Insight Timer* is a great free app that now includes over fifteen thousand guided meditations and courses on learning to meditate. The Teaching Company's Great Courses have several classes on meditation and mindfulness, and you can find many others by searching the internet.

Rick and our daughter Amy have written *The Quick Guide To Mindfulness*. You can download the 18–page PDF version of this short book for free. It contains a four guided meditation, both in transcript and audio forms. To get your free copy, go to the Blog section of our website by going here: https://volweider.com/mindfulness/benefits-of-mindfulness-practice-our-experience/

Shadow work: uncovering your unconscious beliefs, attitudes, and feelings

Years ago, Rick was in a situation where he had to relate to a particular woman on a daily basis for several months. From my perspective, this woman believed she was always right and was never shy about sharing this with others, usually in derogatory ways. Although I was seldom the target of her arrogance, those few times were not pretty. I became increasingly upset and angry during those months. Unfortunately, my anger and frustration did not quickly dissolve after our day-to-day encounters ended, and I no longer had any contact with her. It took years before fully recognizing my shadow was at play.

Carl Jung was one of the first who wrote about the shadow, which we refer to as the Darth-Vader side of the psyche—the dark side, which is rejected from our conscious awareness. Our shadow consists of our thoughts, images, beliefs, attitudes, and behaviors that have been disowned and often projected onto others. Why are certain people so irritating to us? Why do we have specific hot buttons? In some cases, only the shadow knows.

It is hard to work with the shadow since by definition we don't want to see it. However, working with one's shadow can often help control our knee-jerk reactions and help us learn to understand and maybe even appreciate people for whom we had previously felt hostility.

There are numerous ways to work with your shadow and to set it and yourself free, so to speak. Summarized below are the most critical parts of the 3-2-1 Shadow Process found in Ken Wilber and associates' book, *Integral Life Practice*.[3]

The shadow process

Start by thinking of a person with whom you have difficulty. It may be someone you are attracted to but with whom you are at times reactive to or feel irritated, angry, or hurt by. Or choose someone you feel repelled by and feel reactive and up-set with whenever you even think about them. We recommend you record the following process either by writing in a journal or recording yourself talking through the process.

Three: Think through and specifically imagine what disturbs you about this person using vivid detail and as fully as possible. Use third-person pronouns (he, him, she, her) in describing the person you are having difficulty with—like you were talking to someone else about the problems you are having. Talk about what they are doing and also how you think and feel about what they are doing. Take some time to do this before going on to the next step.

Two: Now go into a dialogue (in your mind) with the person with whom you are having a problem using second-person pronouns (you, yours). You might tell them how badly they have hurt, annoyed, or disturbed you, but at some point, begin to ask them questions. You might ask questions like: "why are you doing this? What are you trying to accomplish? What are you telling me? What are you getting out of doing this?

Allow enough time for the person to respond to you (in your imagination) and be sure to write it down or record it in some fashion.

One: Now (here comes the hardest part for most of us), be that person with whom you have been describing and dialoguing. Write or speak in first-person (I, me, my, mine). To identify and take ownership of their characteristics frees you from the patterns of reactivity and increases your self-awareness.

To sum up, whenever we have negative perceptions and conflict with others, shadow work can often help us integrate our feelings and be less emotionally reactive to them. However, this does not apply to victims of abuse and violence. Also, we are not saying that every time you get angry at someone that your devious shadow is to blame. Anger can be a healthy and adaptive emotion, which can signal you to take some action. Sometimes, a cigar is just a cigar.

Formal self-observation

Another way to cut down on knee-jerk type reactions is to use a formal self-observation tool. Of course, you can use this tool for encouraging any change you want. One of the basic principles for fostering change is that you need to know from where you are starting. If you want to lose weight, you first need to find out what you weigh right now. If you want to know if a specific practice, like walking 30 minutes a day, will help you lose weight, you weigh yourself before you start the program and then again a set number of days later.

Using a formal method to monitor specific inner feelings or external behaviors can help in at least two ways. First, having measurements (data) before and after you have used a particular practice can help you determine if that practice moves you toward your goals. Second, when you carefully self-observe a specific behavior or emotional state (and record it in some manner) along with having a particular intent or goal, the actual process of self-observing helps you reach that goal.

In doing the literature review for Rick's master's thesis in the mid-1970s on the reactivity of self-monitoring, he came across several studies that found self-monitoring alone changed how often the observed behaviors occurred. Many of the studies concerned smoking behavior, which the Surgeon General had positively linked to lung cancer about 10-years earlier. The studies typically divided subjects into two groups. One group self-monitored and recorded every cigarette they smoked while the other group did not self-monitor. The group that self-monitored tended to smoke less as the study proceeded. My study replicated these findings (using specific verbal behaviors instead of smoking) and also found that the same verbal behavior could be increased or decreased with self-monitoring by experimentally manipulating if the subject viewed the behavior as either socially valued or devalued. I also found that the more accurately subjects self-observed the larger the increase or decrease in the behavior.

Although extensive journaling is a great method of self-observation, we have found this is too much work for many. The following is a quick and simple self-observation tool.

Self-Observation Form

Score on a 0 to 10 scale with 10 being your ideal

What I want to change	S	M	T	W	T	F	S	Avg
Total of ratings per day								
Avg rating for the day and week								

Pick a few things you would like to change and write them in the first column. We usually encourage people to write what they want to *do*, not what they want to *stop doing*. For instance, in the context of this chapter, you might write, "Listened carefully before responding to others." Look at your list each week and make changes in the items when you want to.

We recommend going over the list each evening sometime before or shortly after you get into bed. In our experience, the main obstacle is remembering to look at the list each day. When using this with client groups, most have found that putting the form on a clipboard with a pen and placing the clipboard on top of one's pillow in the morning has been the best reminder to fill it out. There are several rating apps out there, but we have yet to find one which is flexible and easy to use. Let us know if you discover one you like.

The chart specifies using an 11-point scale with a rating of zero signifying you were a total flop at the item and a 10 representing your ideal behavior regarding the item. If you had a "negative" item like, "Did not smoke," and you did not smoke at all that day, you would also rate that as a 10.

Rating yourself each day provides an opportunity to mentally review your day and how you did on each item. Doing this regularly also makes it more likely that your goals will pop up in your mind throughout the day, often in time to change your behavior on the spot.

Mental rehearsal and stealing behavior

Mental Rehearsal

Healthy *mental rehearsal* is positively engaging your imagination concerning some future event as opposed to worrying about all the bad or negative things that might happen. We often use mental rehearsal, especially when anticipating doing something that feels challenging or is a bit outside our comfort zone. The decision isn't whether or not we *mentally rehearse*. *Our choice* is to either engage in negative, unhealthy, and counterproductive mental rehearsal or a more positive, healthy, and productive mental rehearsal. The mental rehearsal process presented here is rooted in the NLP belief that most of us already have the necessary strengths and skills needed to handle challenging situations. However, accessing and using these strengths can be difficult in certain contexts. For instance, you may be able to express your ideas perfectly well with close friends but find this extremely difficult at work meetings.

The first step of the process is to be aware or mindful of the self-talk and images you are now having when thinking about a specific challenging situation. Notice the feelings they lead to. In your mind's eye make a movie of your behaviors and outcomes that will likely emerge from this way of thinking, imagining and feeling.

After being mindful of your self-talk and imagination and assessing if the feelings and behaviors that stem from them will be helpful, the next step is to think of what *inner resources* you would need to be able to handle the situation in the most productive manner possible. Remember we are talking about *inner*, not *outer* resources. Inner resources are the skills, qualities, and strengths you possess and have been able to utilize in the world at least at times.

Now as vividly as possible, imagine times that you have used those strengths. We recommend seeing this in third-person at first (like you are a camera lens watching yourself). In this view, notice what you are saying to others and how you act toward them. Then go through the scene from a first-person point of view (like you are now seeing out of your own eyes). In this view, notice your thoughts, imagination, and feelings along with the outer realities. Finally, see yourself acting in the challenging situation with these resources, once with a third-person viewpoint and finally with a first-person viewpoint. Then, actually do it.

Stealing behavior

Sometimes we have a clear idea of the thoughts, feelings, and behaviors we want to change and how to change them. Other times, it is hard to clearly picture the desired changes. The strategy below focuses on external behavioral change although one might use a similar strategy to change internal thoughts and feelings. The steps include:

- Identify a new behavior or a change in your current behavior that you would like to implement. If you have difficulty precisely picturing what this new or changed behavior would look like, you can *steal* it from others. Look around in your day-to-day life, TV, movies, or books for someone who is displaying the actions you would like to perform. Carefully watch both the person's gross motor and fine motor behaviors (including facial expression, eye movements, posture, gait, and so on) as well as what they say and how they say it. Now, make a third-person movie (like you are watching on a movie screen) of this person's behavior and notice whatever responses he gets. Make this movie in your mind as vivid and realistic as possible. Use vibrant colors and sharp focusing with as much detail as you can. Now, since you are the director of the movies in your mind, you can run through as many takes as you want. You might want to vary the person's behavior a bit or change the context of the scene for your next take. Keep at this until you find the perfect "take" you'd be happy to include in the final production.

- If you have not done so already, put yourself as the leading actor in your movie and watch yourself act out the behavior (again from a third-person point of view, like you are looking through a camera pointed at you). Allow yourself the number of takes necessary to get it just right. Remember to make your movie as detailed, vibrant, and focused as you can.

- Now, rewind the movie and put yourself in it from the first-person point of view like you are seeing out of your own eyes. You can change your behavior and watch another take of the scene if you are not satisfied with the first one. As you watch your movie, experience it with all your senses as you notice your inner thoughts and emotions.

- Now as you play back the first-person movie, notice

what exterior and interior cues or signals are present that indicate you should engage in this new behavior. External cues might include the content of what another person has said, or the way they said it, or might be some other characteristic of the situation. Internal cues might include your thoughts, feelings, and sensations.

- Finally, think of a situation that might come up in the near future where you would want to use the new behavior. Then, make a mental movie of this situation and your new actions, including the cues that signal you to use this behavior. You can start with a third-person viewpoint but view your movie from the first-person perspective during the last couple of takes.

- Go try it out in your outer life.

- Review how it went. If you are not satisfied with any aspect of your behavior or the outcome, remind yourself that this is precious feedback and start back with step one.

Buy yourself some time

You generally need to use the above practices for a while before you begin to see benefits in emotionally arousing situations. Here we discuss one strategy you can practice any time you are engaged in these types of circumstances.

This strategy involves developing a habit pattern so that when you feel yourself getting upset and angry, you move away from the situation for a while. In some circumstances, it is socially best to say that you need to leave for a few minutes. The bathroom is always a good reason; people rarely quarrel with you about it. If you then leave the bathroom stepping high, almost like you are floating or walking on Flubber, people will assume you've done some pretty important work in there. And hopefully, you have. You have given yourself some time to calm down and relax and think of the most useful response (which sometimes is no response) to whomever and whatever upset you.

Remember that if you buy into the premise of this book, your *best response* is one that is likely to *bring out the best in yourself and others*. If you have been gone five or 10 minutes, the conversation has likely moved on, and you may find it unnecessary to respond to that specific issue, at least at that time.

You can also buy time by saying things like, "Let me think about that for a while." We invite you to spend a few minutes thinking about (and perhaps visualizing or writing down) other things you might say or do to buy yourself some time.

You have likely heard that Success is 90% preparation and 10% perspiration, and earlier we mentioned that Louis Pasteur once said, "Chance favors the prepared mind." The next two chapters move on to other preparatory practices, developing empathy and joy.

4

DEVELOPING EMPATHY

E mpathy is the ability to step into another person's shoes to better understand their perspectives, thoughts, and feelings. Neuroscience is uncovering brain areas and circuits correlated with empathy. One area identified is at the juncture of the parietal, temporal, and frontal lobes. When these areas are damaged, our ability to be empathetic diminishes. Other areas of the brain are correlated with self-centered feelings and behavior. So, it seems we are wired for self-centered behavior in addition to empathy, mutual aid, and social cooperation.

You have probably heard something like, "You've got to take care of yourself if you want to continue to help others." As with almost everything else in life, moderation and balance are essential, at least most of the time. (Oscar Wilde is sometimes credited with saying, "Everything in moderation, including moderation.") Getting in touch with our feelings and being empathetic with others are crucial in bringing out the best in ourselves and others. There is recent neuroscience evidence that being in touch with our own feelings/emotions/ thinking is a prerequisite for empathy with others. But was neuroscience needed to tell us that?

The first two years of life are critical to nurturing our empathic abilities as we strengthen our attachment with our primary caretaker, usually our mother. Marcy Axness, in her book *Parenting for Peace,* eloquently describes how neuronal and emotional development begins soon after conception. To illustrate, here is a passage from her book.

You see, Nature in her wisdom has decreed that while we're in the womb, our brain develops in direct response to our mother's experience of the world. If a pregnant mother's thoughts and emotions are persistently negative, if she is under *unrelenting* stress, the internal message—delivered to the developing baby—is, "It's a dangerous world out there," regardless of whether or not this is objectively true.[4]

You might guess that delivering the message, "It's a dangerous world out there," to a developing human (in or out of the womb) will not do much to help them bring out the best in themselves and others as they mature. Axness tells us that the baby's nervous system cells will change or adapt in response to the perceived threat. Since a detailed discussion of parenting is outside the scope of this book, we heartily recommend reading Dr. Axness's book, which provides comprehensive and research-based parental guidance from before conception to the teenage years.

Assuming everyone reading this book has already been conceived and out of the womb for quite a while, let's turn our attention to what you can do now to increase your empathy toward others, no matter your current status of empathic development.

Let's start with our take on six practices given by Roman Krznaric (in an internet article entitled *Six Habits of Highly Empathic People*), who has investigated both studies on empathy and conducted his own research with highly empathic individuals.[5] We will then discuss some of our ideas.

Be curious about others

Children are naturally curious. Our factory-like school system tends to prescribe what children need to know with little focus on fostering their curiosity. Adults tend to tire quickly of children asking "why?". Many of us replace curiosity with judgment as we mature. Our tendency is to learn some superficial facts about someone and then judge them, often cutting off further inquisitiveness about them.

Think back to your childhood when you were highly curious, perhaps when you were asking a lot of *why* questions. Although adults might not have encouraged your curiosity at that time, you can create an alternate history in your mind and brain. As fully as possible, imagine a parent, teacher, or other adult nurturing your curiosity. Re-play and edit your movie until you are satisfied and feel your curiosity being nurtured.

Being interested in others opens up opportunities beyond our social circles and exposes us to other worldviews and perspectives. It involves trying to understand the other's views and what goes on in their head as you communicate. We encounter strangers daily and making an effort to converse may be a challenge but well worth it. Your life satisfaction is enhanced as a result. Please refer to Chapters 7 and 12 for further discussions concerning cultivating curiosity.

Challenge your stereotypes, prejudices, and look for what you have in common

The last chapter discussed uncovering unconscious beliefs, attitudes, and feelings. As stated above, we often generalize about who someone is after learning just a few things about them, like their race, gender, and religious or political affiliations. These generalizations distance us from appreciating the other's individuality. We limit our perceptions of others by our prejudices and preconceptions. The process divides us rather than uniting us.

One way to work on this is to challenge your stereotypes and prejudices by doing the 3-2-1 Shadow Work outlined in chapter 3.

Another way is to explore what you have in common with the other person. Studies with young children suggest we have inborn tendencies to want to help those we perceive similar to us, and punish (or at least not help) those we perceive unlike us. (We cover these studies in detail in Chapter 9 in the section on inborn prejudice.) Use this knowledge to inspire you to double down on efforts to find commonalities. Also, remember that finding and expressing commonalities with others works both ways in developing relationships.

Directly experience another person's life

Recently Rick talked with a writer for a magazine devoted to living abroad. I told her that I was disappointed that, in my opinion, the magazine rarely presented a balanced view of living in foreign countries, but instead, reported only the upsides and even exaggerating those. She agreed, but in defense of her magazine said that 99 percent of subscribers never left their own country but enjoyed having the magazine on their coffee tables. Although this seemed like a terrible excuse for journalistic bias, the point here is that *relatively few (United States) Americans immerse themselves in the experience of other cultures.* When traveling within one's own country or in a foreign country, most people stay in hotels and visit the major tourist attractions. While there is nothing wrong with this, it tends to insulate the traveler from intimately experiencing the local people and culture. Staying at Airbnbs and hostels typically placed us directly into the local culture since most places listed at airbnb.com are extra rooms or casitas next to the owner's home and are often run by natives of the country or by those who have lived in the country for many years.

Some Airbnbs have space for several couples. These lodgings were among our highlights of traveling. For instance, in Samara, Costa Rica, we stayed at a rustic A-frame cottage with a Canadian couple in their early 30s. We spent about a week sharing the cabin and spent several hours every day talking with each other, covering everything from our childhoods, political and spiritual perspectives, and life aspirations. One day, the four of us talked on and on into the night around a table with candles and mosquito coils lit. It reminded us of late-night talk sessions in college when young and idealistic. This experience also reminded us that while having little control over our physical and chronological aging, we did continue to have considerable influence regarding our mental (imagination), social (caring and sharing), and spiritual development.

Listen and share yourself openly

Open Listening is related to our first point in this section, *Be curious about others*. Open Listening means carefully attending to better understand that person's point of view, feelings, attitudes, and perceptions; it is not listening to judge, criticize, prepare your comeback, or to use the person's words to cut them down and make room for them to believe as you do.

Of course, participating in a relationship requires talking as well as listening. Sharing your own beliefs, points of view, perceptions, and feelings with others provides the opportunity for others to feel and show empathy toward you. It also usually increases your capacity to empathize with others.

Think about how anger often bounces back and forth between two people, growing a bit during each cycle so that at some point, what started as a slightly unkind remark may grow into intense screaming, foul language, and perhaps physical demonstrations of anger. Empathy and empathic behaviors can increase in the same way. Your part is to listen to others openly but also increasingly share yourself openly. Making ourselves vulnerable by revealing our thoughts and feelings to someone is vital in creating a strong empathic bond. Empathy is built on mutual understanding, and removing our own "mask" is part of the process. Please refer to Chapter 7 for a comprehensive discussion of open listening.

Inspire social change

Krznaric encourages us to be a part of social movements that focus on developing empathy in others. He writes, "Just think of the movements against slavery in the 18th and 19th centuries on both sides of the Atlantic. As journalist Adam Hochschild reminds us, 'The abolitionists placed their hope not in sacred texts but human empathy, doing all they could to get people to understand the very real suffering on the plantations and slave ships.' "[6]

Extend empathy as far as you can imagine

Krznaric notes, "We tend to believe empathy should be reserved for those living on the social margins or who are suffering. This is necessary but hardly enough."[7] In addition, most of us feel empathy toward those we care about deeply, especially when they are in a time of crisis.

Research suggests that kids who read a lot of fiction books show more empathy toward others. Watching certain movies and TV shows may have a similar effect. However, the increased use of the imagination when reading provides a unique opportunity to develop our empathic muscle. Also, you have to look hard to find shows and movies that fit this bill. Although we both enjoyed the Jason Bourne movies, it's hard to tout them as lessons in empathy.

In 1970, Milton Friedman, the leader of the Chicago School of Economics, wrote that the sole purpose of business was to make money for its shareholders and that business executives who pursue goals other than making money were, "unwitting puppets of the intellectual forces that have been undermining the basis of a free society."[8] This prime directive was taken extremely seriously by business. Concern and empathy for other stakeholders, primarily consumers of business, became irrelevant.

We will pick on the food industry to explore one example of the effects of the lack of empathy in American business. Since the major food companies' only goal (along with most other industries) was profit for their shareholders, producing the cheapest food (often with the use of chemicals no one can pronounce) that was long-lasting and tasty but not satiating (using lots of fat, salt, and sugar so people would eat more and more) was the order of the day. These orders continue today almost 50 years later.

Many of the major food companies have had great success in this area. According to Michael Pollan's book *Food Rules: An Eater's Manual*, Americans have added 500 calories to their daily diet since 1980, a majority of the calories from snack foods composed mostly of sugar, salt, and fat.[9] In his study of nutrition, Pollan found a lot of controversy concerning the healthiest diets. However, he also found several facts that were not in dispute.

One fact is that people who eat the "Western diet," which generally consists of large amounts of processed foods, meat, refined grains, and added fat and sugar (and not a lot of vegetables, fruits, and whole grains), suffer considerably higher rates of obesity, type 2 diabetes, cardiovascular disease, and cancer than people who eat almost any traditional diet. Pollen states that "Virtually all the obesity and type 2 diabetes, 80 percent of all the cardiovascular disease, and more than a third of all cancers can be linked to this (the Western) diet. Four of the top 10 killers in America are chronic diseases linked to this diet."[10]

Our point here is that the major food industry players showed no signs of empathy, concern, and care for their consumers. Their only concern for consumers was how much they could profit from them by luring them to consume as much as possible of the food and beverages they could produce cheaply. Even today, when the tragic results of their food offerings are apparent to any sane and unbiased person, they continue to invent even more irresistible processed food.

To understand the scale of this problem, we looked at various causes of death in the United States in 2015. During that year, 19,885 Americans died of heroin and synthetic opioid overdoses; 20 were killed by Islamic terrorists; 21 were shot dead by toddlers (a majority of deaths were the toddlers themselves); 15,696 people were murdered, and 38,300 were killed in car accidents. A total of 73,922 deaths in the United States in 2015 were due to narcotic overdoses, murder, Islamic terrorists, toddlers, and cars. Compare that with 536,224 deaths by heart disease and 589,430 deaths due to cancer.[11]

Given Pollan's estimates that 80 percent of heart disease and about one-third of all cancers are linked to the Western diet, the Western diet was implicated in the deaths of approximately 625,450 Americans in 2015. This means that in 2015, the Western diet was linked to about eight and one-half times the number of deaths compared to deaths due to narcotic overdoses, murder, Islamic terrorists, toddlers, and cars. Although America was spending vast resources to deter Islamic terrorists, during 2015, the Western diet helped kill off over 31,000 times the number of Americans killed by Islamic terrorists during that year. We believe that part of the blame falls to American business and its general lack of empathy, care, and concern toward their consumers.

The rise of obesity and chronic diseases in America (and other countries which are moving toward the Western diet) has many causes beyond the greed and lack of empathy of American business. The U.S. government has not been particularly helpful, and we could write several books about taking personal responsibility for one's lifestyle, including food choices, exercise, play, and rest.

However, acknowledging these other factors does not minimize the food industry's myopic drive toward the bottom line while demonstrating little concern toward their consumers.

The main point of the above is to extend our thinking concerning empathy, including how empathy or the lack of it may affect all of us in ways that might not have been considered. Also, the critique of the food industry was presented to demonstrate that empathy is not just an individual affair, but involves groups of people, including business, communities, and nations.

Remember that everyone is cherished by somebody

It might help exercise your empathetic muscle to consider that even people you loathe are loved, revered, cared about, and viewed empathetically by someone. If they can do it, why can't you?

Seek out the unfamiliar

To extend your empathy, seek out new and unfamiliar experiences. Travel to places you've never been. This could mean going to distant places like a foreign country half-way around the world, but it also could mean a 50-yard walk to the neighbor three houses down the street with whom you've never talked.

Of course, just *going* somewhere unfamiliar isn't quite enough to extend your empathy toward others. Soldiers can travel thousands of miles to foreign lands with no resultant growth in their understanding toward the "enemy." You have to go with a mind open to other ways of thinking, living, and viewing the world. This doesn't mean you have to change your principles and beliefs, but you do have to remain open to understand and appreciate these differences. Following are some specific ways to seek out the unfamiliar.

- Go to different churches in your or other communities.
- Watch a movie or TV show you would ordinarily avoid. Documentaries and podcasts can often expand your horizons. Our daughter Amy recently told us about several podcasts that are likely to extend one's empathy. They include *This American Life*, *Hidden Brain*, *No Such Thing As Fish*, *Stuff You Should Know*, *Serial*, and *The Edge Effect*.
- Read a book by an author or in a genre that you haven't before.
- Visit foreign countries.
- Eat in a restaurant serving cuisine with which you are not familiar.
- Visit a neighbor you've only waved at (or not) before.

- Search out the origins of things you like. Often other cultures are involved. Who had the idea for the first pizza?
- Learn another language. Learn and appreciate the beauty and humor of colloquialisms.
- Crash a wedding reception for a couple you've never heard of. Well, okay maybe we are going too far. We'll leave it to you to brainstorm more ideas.

Seek out those you strongly disagree with

According to the Google Dictionary, *confirmation bias* "is the tendency to interpret new evidence as confirmation of one's existing beliefs or theories." Everyone does this. On top of that most of us tend to read and watch sources that mostly confirm what we already think. Conservatives tend to read the Washington Times and watch FOX News while liberals tend to read the Washington Post and watch MSNBC. We recently checked comments on an article from the Washington Times. Of the first 17 commentators, 14 had conservative viewpoints; three had liberal perspectives.

Technology has added even more bias to what we read and see on the internet. Generally, social media gives you more of what you already like or agree with. For instance, Facebook has algorithms to feed you the type of news that you are most likely to look at. In an article on how Facebook determines the news feeds it sends you, Josh Constine writes, "Over time as you interact with the News Feed, Facebook learns what you care about and evolves that understanding if your behavior changes."[12]

So, if you want to widen your scope of understanding and empathizing with others, you've got to manufacture experiences that you currently might not like so much or feel comfortable with. If you now watch FOX News most of the time, check out MSNBC and of course, vice versa.[13] If you now read the *Washington Post*, try the *Washington Times*.

After you can do this for at least a few minutes without going crazy, try dialoguing with a person with whom you disagree. Consider using the general principle used several times in this book by starting with someone you generally respect and with whom you have some minor differences of opinion, and then moving to people with more and more divergent views from yours. Before you do this, it may be helpful to read the section on open versus closed communication in Chapter 7.

Remember that the most fulfilling and durable relationships are mutual in most aspects, including empathetic feelings and behaviors. Reciprocity makes the world turn. I give, you receive; you give, I receive. Each individual cell in our body relates to many other cells, both sending and receiving information through chemical and electrical signals. It seems self-evident to us that a relatively equitable flow of empathy back and forth is crucial for maintaining satisfactory long-term relationships.

Feel and show empathy for the joy of others

Although empathy is the ability to understand and share in the feelings of others, we often narrow our thinking of empathy to sharing feelings of sorrow, loss, and anger. However, don't forget about sharing in others' excitement, happiness, and joy.

Teach your children empathy

It is probably not surprising to learn that in Rick's years of clinical practice with kids, the ones who had the most behavioral and social problems tended to demonstrate the least empathy toward others. I often worked with these children directly at developing empathy but often found it more useful to work with their parents to teach their kids empathy. One strategy is to help kids learn an extended vocabulary for their feelings.

Remember, brain imaging studies have now proven what we already knew...that you have to be aware of your own feelings before you can understand and feel empathy with another's feelings. You and your children can draw faces that represent different feeling states. Also effective is getting out family photos, especially the more candid ones, and discussing what might have been going on and what the people in the photo might have been thinking and feeling. You can then move on to pictures in magazines and books. Of course, the best way for parents to teach their children empathy is to model it by being empathetic toward others, including their kids. It is likely that we have to feel empathy from someone else before we can extend empathy to others.

In the *Roots of Empathy*, Mary Gordon describes a program which teaches empathy to school kids. Part of the process involves the children observing an infant's development over time.

Sheila is the second oldest of nine children. I saw the development of empathy in action. My mom was very nurturing and responsive to our emotions. The three youngest were infants when I was a teenager, and I learned to sense their needs when they were pre-verbal. It was a great training ground to observe and understand their non-verbal communication and their extremely verbal crying spells. Learning to read their moods and responses to comfort them helped me grow in my empathic responses.

As a parent, the process of formally teaching your children empathy will likely help you grow in empathy as well. We once saw a graphic explaining that people learn and remember about 30 percent of what they hear, 40 percent of what they see, 70 percent of what they do, and 90 percent of what they teach others. Most of us learn a lot more by teaching others what we thought we already knew. Lastly, teaching children empathy skills is a way of having a broad impact on society and can bring about fundamental social changes.

5

— ∞ —

CULTIVATE JOY

As we mentioned earlier, one of the most important ways to bring out the best in others is to cultivate your own joy of life. As you do this, you will naturally find and be guided into ways of bringing out the joy in others, which will go a long way in bringing out their best.

Our Mac dictionary defines joy as "a feeling of great pleasure and happiness." Other synonyms include exhilaration, enjoyment, exuberance, euphoria, and bliss.

The phrase "cultivate joy" is used to imply that we can't exactly "construct" joy in our lives like one might build a table. To make a table we might start with specific plans and instructions, maybe a blueprint that is followed precisely. By using the same plans and type of wood as other competent carpenters, our table is likely to turn out looking like the others.

Increasing joy isn't so cut and dried. It's more like planting the right seeds (perhaps after adjusting the soil or searching for the best place to grow them), regularly checking on how things are growing, and making whatever adjustments are needed (like adding more nutrients and water). It might also involve being vigilant in reducing potential damage caused by harmful elements like pests or too much water and sun.

Cultivating joy also implies it takes some time to increase our joy. It is a process that doesn't end, unlike making a table. After you construct the table, you can sit and eat or play cards on it for a long time with very little maintenance—maybe wiping it off once in a while. In contrast, joy is a process needing regular attention although there may come a time when you find yourself constantly and effortlessly experiencing joy. Until then, it probably pays to cultivate joy consciously.

Just as a gardener tries to minimize things that might interfere or block plant growth while maximizing things that promote growth, we can similarly cultivate joy by decreasing what hinders our joy and increasing what adds to it.

Plant spirit medicine

During the early years of the new millennium, Rick attended training, given by Eliot Cowan, to become a plant spirit medicine practitioner. Elliot had received training in five-element acupuncture with Professor J.R. Worsley. After practicing acupuncture for some time, he apprenticed with the Huichol shaman, Don Guadalupe González Ríos. From my point of view, Elliot combined aspects of five-element acupuncture with Huichol shamanism to create (or as Elliot might say, to rediscover) plant spirit medicine.

Part of our training involved learning about the five-elements, by explanatory and experiential methods as well as group sharing. The five elements are an integral part of Traditional Chinese Medicine (TCM). The five elements can be thought of as different aspects of Qi, or the life force.

It is my understanding that in the Chinese system, instead of being material substances, the *elements* are seen as types of energies that continuously interact with each other, directly or indirectly. Each element is associated with different aspects of the personality, emotions, tastes, smells, colors, organs, and meridians in the body, interpersonal relationships, directions, seasons of the year, and in short, with everything that makes the world turn.

For example, winter is associated with the water element, spring with wood, summer with fire, harvest time or late summer with Earth, and fall with metal. Although we all are a unique blend of every element, each of us tends to have a dominant element. Disease is thought to be due to imbalances or dysfunction between in the elements.

In TCM, *joy* is associated with the fire element. Fire and joy are reflected in our *burning* passions, relationships, love and compassion for others, and excitement about life. In the 2014 edition of *Plant Spirit Medicine*, Eliot lists 42 questions to explore our connection with the fire element, which include exploring our relationships with others, how the weather affects us (sunny or cloudy, cold or warm), feelings of happiness and joy, who and what we love and feel loved by, among other questions.

The initial phase in using plant spirit medicine is to thoroughly assess the person, partly to determine the person's dominant element. We were taught to spend a good amount of time discovering what brought joy to the person. Although I had had about two decades of experience assessing clients and had gravitated toward a strengths-based approach early in my career, I had never thought to ask, "What brings you joy?" This simple question gradually changed my therapeutic approach and the manner many clients viewed themselves.

Exercise

Spend some time thinking (and ideally writing) about *what brings you joy*. One way to do this is to sit quietly for 15 to 20 minutes with a notepad to write or cell phone to record every thought you have concerning what brings you joy—both what you have already experienced in your life and things you can imagine experiencing.

The list might include *things* you could own or borrow, what you'd like to *learn*, *places* you might go, *who* you want to *know* or know better, other *activities* you want to engage in, and so on. Don't limit yourself or censor anything; you can go back and do that later if you'd like. For instance, if you imagine that walking on the moon would bring you joy, write it down. When you let the mind go unfettered, you are likely to come up with outrageous and unrealistic ideas; however, these thoughts/images often lead to more practical and doable ideas.

Beliefs that underlie joy and suffering

Before discussing what specifically inhibits and promotes joy, we will explore an underlying factor involved here.

Four or five element theories have been around at least since the ancient Greeks. They vary somewhat in the names of specific elements and if the elements are seen more as energy forces or material substances. The particular ways the elements or energies interact with each other also differs among the theories. However, there is a basic essence that all these conceptualizations have in common. The fundamental principle that they all put forward is the interconnection of all aspects of life and the universe.

However, the worldview for many of us in the Western world conforms to the ideas brought forth during the first several hundred years of the scientific revolution. Seventeenth-century Newtonian physics presupposed individual entities acted upon other discrete entities according to distinct laws. The movement of objects in time and space could be reduced to an equation. Time, space, matter, and energy were considered independent entities that interacted. These ideas worked well in describing the everyday interactions that were observed in the material universe. However, it started to break-down with thought experiments in the early twentieth century and then later with scientific experiments that dug deeper down into the fabric of our universe.

Einstein's theories of special and general relativity upended this notion over 100 years ago. His famous equation $E = mc^2$ basically declares matter and energy interchangeable while his mathematical theory of special relativity implies that space and time are also somehow interchangeable. Heisenberg's theories, including his uncertainty principle, add to the folly of believing in the fundamental separateness and independence of things, including individual humans.

One main point here is that modern physics has concluded that the observer is intrinsically connected to what is being observed and the two cannot be separated.

A higher level of mathematical and abstract intelligence than we possess is needed to appreciate the implications of the theories of special and general relativity and quantum mechanics. Therefore, we offer several quotes by Heisenberg, one of the founders of quantum mechanics, which eloquently and authoritatively express our primary point.

Natural science does not simply describe and explain nature; it is part of the interplay between nature and ourselves; it describes nature as exposed to our nature of questioning. This was a possibility of which Descartes could not have thought, but it makes a sharp separation between the world and the I impossible...

There is a fundamental error in separating the parts from the whole, the mistake of atomizing what should not be atomized. Unity and complementarity constitute reality.[14]

However, it seems that humanity, for the most part, still lives in the delusion of the separateness of things—the idea that there is a sharp separation between me and the rest of the world. It is clear to us that this is one of the underlying roots of much suffering.

Following this way of thinking, joy is the natural result of seeing and feeling the interrelationships and interdependence of all facets of our world. Joy follows the realization that nothing in our universe can exist as a separate entity.

———————

To rephrase the above ideas on a more down-to-earth level, human joy is tied to the perception of our kinship and interrelationship with other people, with all of life, and all other aspects of the world. The solidity and depth of our joy increase as we extend our knowing and feeling of kinship with others and bask in the give-and-take of relationships.

From this vantage point, one can see that most of the emotions that may block our joy, such as loneliness, depression, anxiety, grief, anger and resentment, jealousy, and fear of death, at least partly stem from our lack of true connectedness with others and feelings of being separate from our fellow humans, from all the other life forms on earth, and rest of the universe.

How feelings that inhibit joy are connected to the belief of separateness

Let's discuss how feelings that may hinder joy are connected both to the realities of modernity and a worldview of the separateness of life and the world. We will use loneliness as an example. Loneliness is essentially sadness due to being without companions—human or otherwise. Our Western society with its strong emphasis on individualism—individual rights, individual freedom, and individual wealth, is partly responsible for much of the loneliness in the United States (and increasingly in other countries).

The current political climate and increasing cultural divides also contribute. In our country, whether we should all be responsible for the basic needs and health care of our fellow citizens is still hotly debated, let alone the needs of those who have not followed the rules when crossing our borders, whether their lives depended upon leaving their own countries or not. In sum, both our fervent individualism and current cultural climate foster a view of our separateness.

The decrease of interactions and care among members of many extended families, the growing emotional distance in many neighborhoods, and the devaluing of the elderly are a few more factors that contribute to the loneliness many in the United States feel. Although providing many benefits, exponential growth in technology has reduced much of communication to 256 characters where emojis substitute for personal contact.

It also seems evident that a belief in our separateness can foster loneliness, which hinders joy. It does not seem much of a stretch that other emotions that we commonly believe block joy, such as grief and fear of death, also appear to be connected to the notion of our core separateness.

So what do you do about emotions that inhibit joy?

Working directly with one's inner thoughts, emotions, beliefs, and worldview is a time-honored and effective way to counter negative emotions and change your life for the better. These strategies are covered in previous chapters, especially Chapters 2, 3, and 4. Therefore, the remainder of this chapter focuses mostly on exterior actions you can take to foster joy.

In this section, four stories relate how people have, through specific actions, broken through blockages to reach toward joy. Although each story focuses on one to several joy-blocking emotions, there is usually a wide range of emotions involved in everyone's story.

Grief

A short time ago, Sheila was able to spend several weeks with a close friend, Mary, who is much like a sister, and who had recently undergone horrific trauma. She had been experiencing intense grief and loss for several months. In the face of this, she made a comment that strongly impacted me, "I may always be a sad girl, but I can feel joy." Knowing how hard it is to feel joy when lonely, grieving, and depressed, I was amazed to hear that. I took her to mean that she still felt a constant undercurrent of sadness, but at times, she was able to go beyond this, to moments of joy.

As we spent more time together and as I watched how she managed to get through the day, several things struck me. This included her ability to seek and receive the love of friends and family. Her self-care included being mindful of practical things like nutrition, exercise, sleep, a warm bath, and pacing herself concerning obligations in accord with her current capacities.

Her contemplative life—including prayer, meditation, and mindfulness—have helped her remain aware of the bigger picture and feel more a part of something larger than herself. She has also been able to see herself more as an observer at times, which has helped her problem-solve and carry out practical matters necessitated by her losses. While we were together, she was able to be remarkably honest and realistic about how the changes have impacted her life; she did not sugarcoat them.

Practicing mindfulness has helped her *be in the here-and-now* and accept her changing emotions as well identify and utilize her strengths. By primarily remaining focused in the present, she can cope with one detail after another, cry, laugh, or feel joy at the moment. Her grieving has changed as the weeks pass, and she has increasingly been able to enjoy getting out and engaging in activities. Her continued concern about others has also been instrumental in moving through her grief.

We want to emphasize the actions Mary has been taking to help her go through the grieving process. She has sought out friends, at first arranging to be with one or two close friends at a time. Besides emotional love and support, these friends also gave invaluable logistical support in legal, financial, and organizing matters. She also identified and acted on ways to nurture and strengthen herself, such as taking warm baths, eating well, getting enough sleep, and pacing herself. Her continued meditation practice has helped her be more mindful throughout the day. This has been helpful for both controlling emotions and seeing things more clearly, which has enhanced her problem-solving abilities. It appears that getting out and connecting with others that, while painful at times, has helped her move along in her grieving process.

Abuse/anger/guilt

Sheila's friend Jan demonstrated the true meaning of forgiveness. Her mother raised Jan after her stepfather died when she was nine years old. Her stepfather had been loving and supportive, but after his death, her mother began severely abusing her—both emotionally and physically. Her mother also directed her younger brother to participate in the abuse. I was surprised when Jan told me that in her thirties, she became a caretaker for her mother who had health and financial problems. We talked about how she was able to forgive and provide care for her mother.

Jan said that forgiveness happened in several stages for many years. She had decided that she did not want to be a hateful and angry person and realized the importance of releasing herself from the effects of her mother's abuse. When Jan began to help her mother, she struggled with her feelings. Gradually, as she developed increased self-worth, she was able to take a wider view and realize how mentally sick her mom had been. After several years of caring for her mother, her mom told her why she had always hated her.

Jan learned that her mother had been extremely jealous because she believed her stepfather loved Jan more than he loved her. Although it was devastating to Jan to find out her mom had always hated her, her mother's admission helped Jan redefine herself and realize that she was not to blame for being abused. Subsequently, she bravely talked to her brother about this, which enabled them to become close and mutually supportive with each other.

Despite years of being abused, Jan decided that she wanted to be a kind and loving person toward others. The nurturing she received from her step-father for her first nine years of life was likely a significant contributor to her ability to make this decision. Having made this decision and knowing that her mother was sick, could not take care of herself, and was in desperate financial straits led her to decide to assist in her mother's care-taking.

Besides becoming a caretaker for her mother, which lasted several years, she also openly listened to her mother. Her open listening brought out more personal stories from her mother, some of which her mother likely never told another person. Although hearing these things from her mother was painful for Jan at times, what she learned eventually became the basis of further healing. Lastly, Jan's actions in contacting and re-forming her relationship with her brother have brought healing and connection.

Depression, resentment, and drug addiction

Many years ago, Sheila was privileged to meet a remarkable man. During Steve's early years, he experienced extreme abuse from his parents. Besides emotional and physical abuse, his parents often tried out new batches of drugs on him to test their effects and safety. He was addicted to drugs by the time he was six years old. In his late teens, he went to prison for crimes he committed while on drugs and of which he had no recall. He did not doubt he committed the crimes because he was caught in the act. He served 25 years in prison.

During his first 22 years in prison, he was profoundly depressed and often suicidal. Then, a compassionate guard intervened after his failed suicide attempt. The guard's genuine and continued concern was the first time Steve felt he mattered to someone. Steve began to feel a flicker of hope and self-worth. He used the last three years in prison to access educational classes, which included learning several practical trade skills.

Upon his release, he experienced significant challenges, including living in poverty, staying drug-free, and finding work. However, he gradually progressed. As Steve adjusted to life outside prison, he used his new skills to help anyone he saw who needed help. Although he had no money to give others, he would repair cars broken down on the roadside and help fix things for others in any way he could. Steve didn't know most of the people he helped. He never saw many of them again, but quite a few became friends.

Steve told me that he felt the best when he could "give back" and that he learned self-worth through helping others. He credited his happiness and joy during the 15 years after his prison release to his compassionate actions toward others in assisting them however he could.

Anxiety

Due to her genetic predisposition and stressful life situations, Elizabeth developed moderate anxiety in her early twenties. When Elizabeth is feeling stuck or anxious at home, she often goes outside. She pays attention to her surroundings, which helps ground her in the present moment. Being out in nature often feels healing and reassuring to her. This helps her feel she is part of something bigger than her life situations.

Elizabeth has found throughout the years that she often can leave anxiety at the door when she engages in various social situations. She is also likely to move toward joy in these situations.

Elizabeth recently came home after hours of frustrating doctors' appointments. By the time she arrived, she was even more anxious and frustrated. Adding to this, she felt added pressure because she and her husband had invited a friend over for dinner. Initially, she felt this was more than she could handle. After an extended hug from her husband, she was able to start cooking. Soon after she began, their friend arrived and began telling a long and involved story. She found herself responding to elements of his story as she increasingly focused on interacting with their friend. It was helpful that aspects of his story were funny, which led to humorous responses from Elizabeth and her husband.

Elizabeth sometimes forces herself to engage in social situations when she is feeling anxious or sad. For instance, she might take her dog to the nearby dog park where she knows she will encounter other adorable dogs and their friendly owners, many of whom she now knows. (There are many advantages to pet ownership.)

Since Elizabeth is generally an extrovert, these strategies to minimize anxiety and maximize good feelings, including joy, are more natural for her to employ than they would likely be for more introverted persons.

Elizabeth practices formal mindful meditation in addition to striving to be mindful in valued activities such as artwork, working with her clients, and interactions with her husband. However, when she is feeling anxious, she usually tries to change the scenery by going outside and enjoying nature or arranging a social connection. She plans to enroll a class or two or participate in an organization she is interested in, so she will have more social opportunities. Although she often moves into external, physical activity when she is anxious, her ongoing meditation practice undoubtedly helps her when attempting to move from one state of mind to another.

The value of negative emotions

Most of the above stories describe emotions that stemmed from unthinkable situations, and it's hard to see how their suffering could have been necessary in any way. However, negative emotions themselves may, at times, serve a useful and essential function.

For example, in five-element Chinese medicine, *anger* is the emotion associated with the wood element. Wood is also associated with springtime and the color green. Spring brings growth and new life. When something interferes with one's growth and development, anger can be a natural, adaptive, and healthy internal response. Anger is a sign we need to deal with the situation in some way.

Letting anger brew inside and fester without taking action is as unhealthy as responding with inappropriate rage, which often escalates the situation along with our anger. Sometimes, external actions can resolve conditions related to our anger while other times most of the work is internal.

In other words, many emotions that we might consider to be negative are natural, healthy, and adaptive when seen as signals of a disturbance. These emotions become unhealthy when allowed to brew and perhaps morph into more intense and permanent thoughts and feelings. Although the passage of time and engaging in other things can sometimes be enough to move on from negative emotions, we need to consider to more actively deal with the ones that linger.

The seeds of joy

You may have noticed that although the last section seemingly focused on "negative" emotions that hinder joy, the stories of healing dealt mostly with internal and external actions that foster joy while reducing or morphing the "negative" emotions. In other words, most of the elements in the stories did not illustrate meeting the negative emotions head-on. A more direct approach for working with emotions can be found in our discussion of shadow work in Chapter 3. If you are interested in other strategies that deal with the obstacles to joy more directly, check out *The Book Of Joy*. We will tell you more about our impressions of this book at the end of this chapter.

The primary commonality in the above stories is that each person sought connection with other people. Two stories em-

phasized how joy can be found in compassionate actions toward others while the other two stories emphasized the healing properties of different types of connections with others,
together with self-care. There is a large body of research of the
benefits of both compassionate acts toward others as well as
human connection in general.

Meaningful and productive interactions with others can
take on all sorts of forms. We think most human interactions
that incorporate mutual caring and respect can be seeds of joy.

Is joy only about connecting with other people?

No. Although this chapter and much of this book are focused
on connecting with others as the primary road to joy, there are
other pathways. We have focused on connecting with others,
at least partly in response to the domination of individualism
and materialism in our society as well as the disregard and
disrespect of those who disagree with others or see others as
different from them.

You might think we have overreacted, overreached, and
overstated the *connection with others theme*. We are just bal-
ancing the books a bit.

To state this a bit differently, all of us are individuals and
yet are part of something much bigger—two sides of the same
coin. Honoring both is extremely important at all scales of
life. For example, physically we are composed of trillions of
individual cells. The integrity of each cell is essential to our
continued existence.

Equally important is the ability of each cell to interact, cooperate with, nourish, and be nourished by other cells and

components of our bodies. Even more critical is the miraculous ability of groups of cells to organize to form other entities, like tissues and organs, that carry on functions that individual cells or even clumps of cells could never do. In our Earthly existence, it can't be every cell or every person solely for themselves. On the other hand, every cell and every person needs to maintain their individuality while contributing to something much greater.

The other major pathway to cultivate joy

While a large part of cultivating joy has to do with interacting with, serving, and acting compassionately toward others, an equally large part is valuing and developing our own unique desires and burning passions. Joseph Campbell famously told us, "Follow your bliss." Similarly, in a recent YouTube video, Matthew McConaughey says, "Joy is the feeling we have for doing what we are fashioned to do."[15]

Although we are stubbornly sticking with the idea that joy and bliss proceed from our connections with the world, this connection can be with other people, animals, ideas, places, aspects of ourselves, and every other thing you can imagine and not yet imagine.

Back to the four stories in this chapter, Mary has a passion and knack for gardening. Jan is crazy about dogs and has taken in many that were homeless. Steve was passionate about taking things apart and putting them back together in a much-improved fashion. Elizabeth is a fantastic artist who finds bliss in drawing animals that often seem to look as alive as the real thing.

Please go back to the joy list you made at the beginning of the chapter or start this list if you have not already done so. Maybe you will have a few more things in mind after getting through this chapter. Keep the list handy and add to it. Think about it, experiment. You might be surprised what can bring you joy.

The book of joy

We can't leave this chapter without heartily recommending a recent book about joy that we consider a masterpiece. During April 2015, Archbishop Desmond Tutu and His Holiness the Dalai Lama spent a week together at the Dalai Lama's home in Dharamsala, India. Throughout the week, they celebrated His Holiness's eightieth birthday and discussed how joy can be cultivated in the face of suffering. The interactions of these two men, who while often kidding each other concerning their divergent views of spirituality, demonstrated abundant loving kindness toward each other.

Their conversations are presented and amplified in *The Book of Joy*, coauthored by these two men and Douglas Abrams. For us, this book is the most touching, informative, and practical discussion in print about how to cultivate joy. The book both analyzes obstacles to joy while providing specific practices to overcome the obstacles and develop what they refer to as the eight pillars of joy. We strongly encourage you to read their entire book and to try out a number of the practices presented.

SECTION

THREE

SPECIFIC STRATEGIES TO BRING OUT THE BEST IN OTHERS

H aving a healthy mindset (Section One) and engaging in the practices to prepare your mind and brain (Section Two) are essential components in bringing out the best in yourself and others. However, these mostly interior/mental activities will have limited value for others unless you take action in the exterior/physical world.

This section of seven chapters provides the specific strategies to bring out the best in yourself and others. Chapter 6 briefly discusses what not to do while the remaining chapters explore particular actions to take. Many of these strategies are easy to talk about but considerably harder to do consistently. Like many things in life, they are *easier said than done*. The goal is not perfection, but progress toward the ideal of always bringing out the best in yourself and others.

However, before getting into specifics, we'd like to offer a very general and metaphorical way to think about bringing out the best in others. In working with parents, Rick often used a gardening analogy to help explain different parenting styles.

The *bonsai gardener* has a specific image in mind and shapes the tree to fit this mental image just as the *bonsai parent* tries to fashion their child's thoughts, feelings, and actions to conform precisely to the parent's desires and expectations. The *free-form* gardener throws out some seeds and then "lets it happen." *Free-form* parenting involves seeding to get the child started and then minimal sustenance to keep the kid alive while providing little or no nurturance and guidance.

The *gardener* who *nurtures* his plants while *providing necessary boundaries* provides the plants with the needed nutrients and keeps out elements (too much water, weeds, etc.) that might harm the plants. *Nurturing with boundaries* parenting attempts to give children the caring and encouragement needed to unfold in their own way while providing limits to keep them safe and develop capacities to care for themselves and others.

We are obviously in a different role as parents to our children than the roles we take with others in our lives. However, that same spirit of nurturing the natural development of others, as opposed to trying to shape them to our image of who and how they should be, best expresses our goal in bringing out the best in others as well as in ourselves.

6

WHAT NOT TO DO

Both of us have a strong theoretical bias to focus on what we *want*—including material things, circumstances, and our thoughts, feelings, and actions—*not* on what we *don't want*. However, as with about anything, there are some exceptions. Sometimes, negatively stating an instruction gets to the point much quicker and may more likely prevent an unfortunate result, as in "Don't touch the stove's coils when they are red!"

Our list of what not to do follows. There also might be some exceptions to these *do nots* in specific circumstances.

Don't read this book with focused attention and astute self-reflection, and then do nothing

You've got to apply these ideas, processes, and strategies by taking action in the material world to get the most from this book.

Don't ask many closed-ended questions

Although questions asking for *yes* or *no* answers or *short* answers (like, "How old are you?") are fine on a limited basis, they usually don't give you much information about who the person really is and don't engender deeper communication. When trying to bring out the best in others, ask more *open-ended* questions as discussed in Chapter 8.

Don't do other things like

Playing with your cell phone, listening with your earbuds, or playing with your spinner (a fidgety toy) while trying to connect with others. Enough said.

Don't interrupt others when they are talking

Often the content of what others are saying reminds us of something we'd like to tell them, and we think by waiting, we will forget all about it. However, think about the message this might be sending to others. Maybe something like, "What I have to say is a lot more important than your blabbering." Of course, there are exceptions:

- This is usually not a big deal when you know the person well, and you don't do it often.
- A large coconut is about to fall on the person's head.

- You suddenly have to use the bathroom.

Don't talk about yourself the majority of the time.

Don't dispense with advice until you understand the other person and his or her situation

When you understand more fully, you may realize giving advice will likely not be as helpful as other actions.

Don't listen with the intent of picking apart what they are saying

Sometimes you may find yourself thinking, *How the flying feathers can you think that way?* However, saying this will not likely bring out their best. When you find yourself thinking this way, ask yourself how you can best investigate their ways of thinking so you can begin to understand. This is covered in detail in Chapters 7, 8, and 10.

Don't blame others for your feelings

Don't say, "You made me feel angry when you..." Instead, take responsibility for your feelings by saying something like, "I felt angry when you..." Please see Chapter 11 for more on what to do in these situations.

Don't spread malicious gossip

Common enemies and frustrations can bring out cooperation among people. A favorite way for many to interact with others is gossiping about mutual acquaintances, at times judgmentally. Gossiping is a major path of bonding with others and is probably as old as human language. However, judgmental and hateful gossiping rarely helps bring out the best in ourselves and others. Many people seem to delight in going into detail concerning their frustration with others. Generally, encouraging this behavior is not constructive, and we usually don't recommend matching another person's frustration with other people.

However, a possible exception is if you intend to *match* the frustrated behavior to establish rapport and then to help the person find a more helpful perspective. This means you might first mirror the other person's frustration with someone by talking about your frustration with someone else. You then might try to widen their perspective by talking about how you were able to come to an agreement with the person or somehow adjust the situation or your thoughts and attitudes in a way that relieved your frustration. Chapter 10 goes into detail concerning matching (*pacing*) others as well helping them develop different perspectives and behaviors (*leading*).

If someone is telling you how upset they are at another person and then begins gossiping about her, you could validate their feelings toward that person without validating or joining in on the gossiping.

While writing this chapter, our daughter Sara reminded us that in middle school she was often upset when her friends gossiped about each other. Sara remembered talking with her mother about this at the time. Sheila had suggested that when she heard one friend gossiping about another, she could say, "Oh that's funny, they always say the nicest things about you." Sara said she remembered that when she used that phrase, it quickly shut down the gossiping. Of course, we'd recommend saying something like this only if there was at least some truth behind it.

One last thought on gossip: Have you ever listened to someone who is always complaining and gossiping about others and then wondered what that person tells others about you when you're not around?

7

PRACTICE OPEN LISTENING SKILLS

This chapter is placed first among the specific skills needed to bring out the best in others. It is a critical skill that provides a foundation for all the other strategies and it has been one of the hardest things for us to do well in our marriage. We have been aware of the importance of this idea, taught it professionally, and practiced it reasonably well with others, including our daughters, for decades. However, it has been a struggle to do it consistently with each other. Although we have made considerable progress, this skill will probably challenge us until death do us part.

What is open listening?

Whenever you listen to another person, at any one moment,

you can take an *open* or *closed* approach. When you are engaged in an *open* approach, you are curious and interested in what that person thinks, believes, and feels.

You are like an explorer encountering a territory for the first time, an adventurer. You are not trying to change anything about the territory but discovering what it's really like. You may begin to develop some understanding of how the various parts of the territory interact and fit together. You appreciate the trees, the rocks, and the wildlife. Some look familiar; you have seen similar kinds in other places. But some appear completely different from any you've seen before. You've seen waterfalls before, but this one is higher and involves more water than you've ever seen or imagined. And then a magnificent double rainbow appears, exceptionally bright and colorful.

Now you don't say to yourself, "This isn't what I expected; it's not right. What can I do to change it into what I expect and feel comfortable with?" But you might say, "This isn't what I expected; Wow!" Your discovery enthralls you, and you feel in awe—of God, nature, life, etc. You don't judge, especially in a condemning way, and you certainly don't try to change it. You are there to appreciate and learn *what is,* not create *what (you think) should be.*

Likewise, when you openly listen to a person, you are an explorer of their attitudes, beliefs, values, ways of perceiving, thoughts, feelings, and more. Although you may disagree with some of their beliefs, values, etc., you spend little energy on this. Instead, you devote your energy to understanding what it is like for them, developing empathy for them in their particular circumstances (which includes their exterior situation, their past, their mind, their brain, and possibly even their Spirit).

When you listen openly, you are not thinking about your

rebuttal. For a time, you give up comparing their beliefs to your own beliefs. You are more interested in understanding what their beliefs really are and perhaps how they came to those beliefs. You ask questions to clarify and better understand, not to help them think and feel correctly as you do.

Sheila remembers visiting an aging uncle with Alzheimer's at a nursing home. Uncle Hershel was talking with two other residents. They seemed engaged with each other on some level; however, the content of what they said in response to one another appeared to have nothing to do with what the other person had just said. Although they seemed incapable of actually understanding and responding to the content of each other's words, their non-verbal communication (including tone of voice, body language, and timing of their responses) appeared complementary, and their conversation came across as fostering mutual enjoyment, connectedness, and maybe even understanding on some levels. In some ways, they were models of open communication.

What is closed or defensive listening?

Closed or defensive listening focuses on inspiring (or perhaps demanding) others to get their heads on straight—like yours. You listen just enough so that you can come back at them with a witty, thought-out counter argument to their position on things. In closed listening, you are focused on *defending your position* as soon as you realize the other person doesn't agree with yours. Therefore, we also call this *defensive listening* or *defensive communication*.

With closed/defensive listening, your questions become tools to critique others, get a sense of where they err, and get them on the right path. Your focus is defending your position and then getting them to see the light. You don't need to know much about their position; why spend time trying to understand something that is just plain wrong? When you listen to others in a closed manner, you are subtly or not so subtly trying to gain dominance of your ideas and beliefs in the relationship.

Quickly making judgments of the other person's responses, comparing them to your own thoughts, and focusing on what you can say to defend your position and change theirs is the essence of *closed/defensive listening/communication.*

We believe that in close relationships when two people vehemently disagree, both parties often maintain a defensive posture in "listening" to the other. After listening to a few words and finding disagreement, the listener starts fashioning his rebuttal, often beginning his refutation before the other person has finished her thought. The other person often responds similarly and so on until the "conversation" fizzles out or grows to an uproar with more than words thrown about and someone angrily stomping off. Some people mutually or separately decide to avoid certain topics to keep the peace and eliminate discomfort. Some decide to break off the relationship entirely. Others appear to enjoy the uproar—let the games begin.

Ideally, in a conversation between two people, at any one moment, one person is speaking, and the other is listening. When interrupting or quickly responding to another person, we are often defending our position, unless we are asking clarifying questions to understand that person better.

The *open/closed* dimensions apply primarily to the listening part of the conversation. Although we have presented *open/closed* as an "either/or"—you are either listening in an open or closed (defensive) posture, it is actually a continuum where open and closed are at opposite ends. So, you can be mostly curious and trying to understand and identify with the other person's viewpoint and at the same time being just a bit judgmental and preparing your response containing some degree of *defending your position*. Or you can mostly focus on defending your position while giving just a bit of attention to understanding theirs.

Why practice open listening?

If you want to bring out the best in people, practice open listening as much as practically possible. We firmly believe that when feeling genuinely listened to and accepted, one is most open to change. Most of us tend to hunker down when feeling verbally attacked or rejected—the opposite of feeling accepted and valued. We hunker down to keep what we've got (our positions) and not let in anything new that might conflict with our views. On the other hand, when feeling accepted and valued, we are more likely to consider other viewpoints and are more open to modifying our own.

With a little introspection, you can test out this idea for yourself. Think about when you have been self-critical, when you have intensely judged your own thoughts, feelings, or actions negatively. You are disappointed with yourself. You feel stupid and embarrassed, and then to top it off, you might feel foolish for feeling these ways. Does this type of self-criticism and self-loathing help you change?

By genuinely accepting ourselves (including our limitations, excesses, blind spots, shadow elements, etc.) we are open to change. It may seem a bit paradoxical. If we deeply accept ourselves, why would we want or feel a need to change? When our ego fully accepts who we are now, it can step out of the way and allow for our deeper selves (maybe even Spirit) to make an appearance. The deep self is allowed to run the show for a while, leading to significant and fundamental changes.

Another way to look at this seeming paradox is to recognize that most of us get into a defensive posture when feeling criticized or attacked. The essence of our defense is to let in nothing new in order to keep (defend) what we have. This is an anti-change posture, which while preserving what is there, allows no room for growth. On the other hand, when feeling accepted and valued, one can let down this defensive posture, which opens the door to growth. Your job is to do your best to understand and respect the beliefs, thoughts, and feelings of others, which opens up the possibility of change.

How to listen more openly

If you have been convinced that bringing out the best in people involves listening to them openly, how do you do it? Remember that our first reaction is to defend our position, which is the essence of a closed/defensive posture. So it takes some work and perseverance to learn how to listen openly, especially for intimate partners and other long-term relationships. The following suggestions will only help if you consistently practice them. Just reading about them won't do much. In addition to practicing the general preparatory exercises in

Chapter 3, the following provides specific guidelines.

Pay attention to your reactions

You probably do not always react defensively to everybody all the time. If you do, note that and move on down the list. Most likely, you tend to get defensive (and in a closed listening mode) when specific people talk about particular things. *Take note of who you usually openly listen to.* Maybe it's your priest or minister or maybe not. Perhaps it's a trusted friend. It might be an authority figure you enjoy reading, watching, or listening to.

Then, consider the reasons you tend to stay open when listening to them (or reading their material). Do you respect them because they are older? Does their societal position come into play? Is their gender or race involved? Or Is it that you already agree with everything they say? Then consider whom you tend to listen to in closed mode. You may find your children, parents, spouse, or an ex-spouse will top the list.

Then investigate the type of topics or situations involving that person that stir up your defenses. You will probably discern a few (or more) hot issues. Reflect on why these people and topics or situations bring out your closed listening mode. After you have reflected on past events, *start paying attention to your current interactions with others.*

Take this information and apply the mental rehearsal and stealing behavior strategies covered in Chapter 3. The goals in practicing these strategies are to more quickly recognize when you are moving into defensive listening and then to better direct yourself back to listening openly.

Listen to or watch presentations of topics by people with whom you are likely to disagree

You might start with those you disagree with a little and move to those you with whom you think you will strongly disagree. If you're a Republican, listen to MSNBC, or if you are a Democrat listen to Fox news. Now you can always put them on pause and respond defensively for as long as you like. Let them say another half-sentence, put them on pause again, and so on. However, we recommend practicing open listening to these presentations. Instead of focusing on refuting everything they say, practice focusing and understanding what they are saying and the reasons, logic, and facts as well as the feelings and worldviews behind what they are saying. Think about the clarifying questions you might ask if you were involved in a one-on-one discussion with them. Notice how you feel as you conduct this exercise.

Visualize that you are talking with someone about something with which you have had difficulty staying in an open listening mode

See (and hear) yourself with the ability to recognize that you are starting to go into defensive listening style but are quickly able to refocus to a more open approach. You might see yourself as a Pulitzer Prize-winning journalist who is interviewing a principal source for an important story. You see yourself striving to gather information, so you can tell the story in an unbiased way. Alternatively, you can see yourself as the scientist or the explorer discussed at the beginning of this section. Also, note our extended discussions of *visualization* when using mental rehearsal and stealing behaviors in Chapter 3.

Each time you act on your intent to hold back on interrupting someone or suppress immediately firing back a defensive response, you tend to decrease the likelihood or at least the intensity of your defensive thoughts and emotions in the future

It's like you are telling yourself by your inaction that those defensive thoughts and feelings are not all that important right now. You don't need to act on them immediately, so it's not important to be having those defensive thoughts and feelings right now. It's unlikely this will be a one-shot fix, but over time, you will see your interior defensive postures shrinking.

Cut short any defensive responses the moment you realize this is what you are doing

As discussed above, if you do this regularly, you will begin to reduce the number of times you respond defensively, and over time, the interior aspects of your defensiveness (feelings, thoughts, and judgments) will also decrease.

Remember that suspending your defensive thoughts, feelings, and actions doesn't mean that you are giving up those beliefs and values that are behind them

It doesn't even mean that you can't fully express your beliefs, values, and thoughts to this person later at a later time. You are just suppressing the urge to fire back immediately with a defensive response while remaining in an open listening mode.

Use a self-monitoring tool, like the one in Chapter 3, to record your success at listening openly

In that chapter, we recommended rating yourself on a few specific items you want to change on a 0 to 10 scale. Since we prefer items that express what you want (instead of don't want), your item might be "Remained in an open listening stance in conversations." A *10* would signify that you remember keeping an open listening posture during every conversation you had that day. A *0* would mean that during every conversation you remember that day, you listened to only a few words from others before focusing on and giving your rebuttal. In other words, you maintained an entirely closed or defensive listening manner throughout the entire day. As discussed in chapter 3, self-monitoring, along with an intent to change, can be powerful change tools over time.

If you are sharing this book's ideas with a spouse or close friend, it can be helpful to work on specific strategies together

Regarding the present discussion, you would first both agree that it makes sense to practice more open communication with each other. Applying the above strategy, you could monitor both your own closed and open listening behavior and that of your partner during the day. At the end of the day, you could rate how you think you both did toward each other.

You would then discuss your ratings with each other. An important consideration is that you both agree in advance to try your best to stay open to your partner's comments during this discussion.

The benefits of practicing this exercise include the power of self-monitoring to change behavior and the reality-check with your partner's ratings of your listening skills. As a bonus, as you and your partner process this exercise together, it gives both of you the opportunity to practice open listening skills on the spot and in a context that you may find challenging.

Many people may find it difficult to resist the urge to jump in prematurely to defend their position before thoroughly exploring the other person's viewpoint and beliefs

Another exercise or practice you can do with a partner is to use an external timer, like a kitchen or cell-ph1one timer, to assure you both have a certain amount of time to relate your viewpoint before your partner launches their rebuttal. For starters, you might set the timer for five minutes. If your partner is the one explaining his or her thoughts at that time, you would practice open listening (and perhaps open questioning) until the timer dings. At that point, you can mutually decide for your partner to continue another five minutes or for you to start expressing your viewpoint. Of course, this exercise only works if both partners get a chance to share their views in addition to practicing open listening.

Ask questions

When we want to understand more about a specific aspect of the natural environment than can be obtained from our five senses, we often use devices and technologies that expand the abilities of our senses. For example, binoculars, telescopes, microscopes, MRIs, and CT scans provide a clearer picture of what is going on. To better understand another person's viewpoint, the simplest method is to ask questions.

However, asking questions can also be used as a somewhat disingenuous method to get others to discover the error of their ways and come around to your way of thinking, in other words, to defend your position. Although asking questions designed to get others to re-think their views can be valuable, it is not an open listening strategy. Nevertheless, these types of questions might be helpful for another to understand your point of view better after you have connected with them through open listening.

8

COMMUNICATE PROACTIVELY AND SEARCH FOR DEEPER CONCERNS

Communicate proactively

This chapter is mostly applicable to situations where you have ongoing contact with others, including family members, close friends, and people you work with. However, you can also apply these ideas and strategies whenever helping anyone figure out solutions to a problem.

One of the habits, detailed in Steven Covey's classic book, *The Seven Habits of Highly Effective People*, is to be *proactive*. In some ways, this is opposite to the saying, "If it's not broke, don't fix it." This may work well in some situations but fail miserably in others. For instance, as a poor graduate student, Rick would go with the premise that if his car was still running, he didn't need to worry about stopping at a gas station.

In relationships, there are at least two ways to work proactively. The first is to think ahead and maintain things, so they don't break—or to talk about possible difficulties, so later you don't get into a big argument with your partner or kids concerning the issue. For example, before getting married, it's usually best to talk about the desire (or non-desire) to have kids in the marriage. If you and your potential partner vehemently disagree on this issue, maybe this isn't the marriage for either one of you. At the least, it would be great to come to an agreement that satisfies you both before marriage, while keeping in mind that we all can change our desires and opinions as life goes on. The best way to find agreement is to explore each other's beliefs, opinions, feelings, and concerns about the issue.

Another way to work proactively in relationships is to wait awhile to fix what is broken until things have settled down a bit. In other words, do not talk about a disagreement in the *heat of the battle*. Most of us tend to lose quite a few IQ points (especially social intelligence points) when upset or angry. We often attempt to solve problems in this state because that is when the problem or situation presents itself. Often, ill-thought-out proclamations are made by one or both parties, things often escalate, and the process tends to alienate instead of unite.

Many times the deep concern is overshadowed by superficial quasi-solutions. For instance, parents may insist their son must be home by 10:00 PM. Usually, arguments ensue, and each party adamantly defends their position, which prevents a more in-depth look into the parent's or son's concerns.

However, if the parents investigate their stance more thoroughly, they may find their deeper concerns are that their son is safe and that they know he is safe. In turn, the son may realize that he feels foolish leaving before his friends, and he doesn't get much chance to hang out with them at other times. At that point, they might negotiate a later curfew with the provision the son calls (or more likely texts) by 10:00 PM, telling his parents where he is, whom he is with, and when he will be home.

Deep concerns are almost never uncovered in the heat of the battle when emotions are running hot or some action needs to be taken immediately. We have often counseled parents and couples to wait until the issue doesn't matter (at the moment) before discussing it. Some issues may involve one-time matters and need no discussion at all. However, many problems keep resurfacing in one way or another and need to be worked out. Again, issues can be best worked out when it isn't an issue at the moment, which usually means both parties are relatively calm, can think clearly, and are more likely to be open and curious about the other's viewpoints, thoughts, and feelings. We are also more likely to discover our own deeper concerns when we are not upset and angry.

So how do you become more proactive in searching for mutual solutions to problems and disagreements? One method is to stop trying to solve difficulties during the heat of the battle as soon as you recognize this is what you are doing. The 10 strategies reviewed in Chapter 7, which concern how to listen more openly, also apply here.

Using a self-observation tool, as described in Chapter 3 can be helpful. Using a negative item (describing what you don't want to do) might make sense here. The item might read something like, "Did not try to solve problems when upset or angry." Written positively, it might read, "Worked at finding solutions with others only when calm."

Search for deeper concerns

As just mentioned, deep concerns are seldom uncovered when one or both parties are angry and upset. As described above, many curfews and other restrictions that parents give their children are based on the underlying concerns that their child is safe and staying out of trouble. Of course, most parents don't just want their children *to be* safe; they want to *know* that they are safe. "Be home by 10:00 PM" doesn't leave a much room for creative negotiation while "I want to know that you are okay and safe," leaves a lot of room.

In many interpersonal disagreements, both parties individually come up with a specific solution (such as, "Be home by 10:00") to handle a deeper concern, which they may not even realize they have. They then stick to this specific solution while forgetting the deeper issue or concern if they ever realized it at all.

Their child often reacts to this command with her own solution, something like, "I'll come home when I'm ready to." Parent and child then argue back forth on the surface issue, often escalating in anger and volume. Both parent and child are usually listening defensively, which is a significant reason deeper concerns never come up. Some children learn to nod in agreement with their parents and then do what they want to do. Of course, all this applies to all types of long-term relationships, not just the parent-child type.

Several years ago, Rick spent an entire therapy session discussing a disagreement between an 11-year-old boy and his mother. The argument concerned how often the boy took a shower. Mom thought he should take a shower at least every other day, and her son thought every other week should be sufficient. This argument had been going on for several years and was seriously straining their relationship. With some prodding, mom expressed her deeper concerns succinctly. She talked about the need for good hygiene, how all sorts of nasty skin problems can occur without it, and how friends might become increasingly scarce due to his smell and appearance.

It took considerably longer for her son to talk about his deeper concerns. Like most of the kids in my practice, I assumed adults seldom asked him what was behind his surface concerns. He finally said that he didn't like lying on his pillow with wet hair.

We switched to problem-solving (or solution gathering) mode, and mom and son came up with five ways to address their mutual deeper concerns. They settled on the son using mom's hair dryer after taking an evening shower. A few weeks later, during the next session, they reported he was now taking showers with no problem.

How to Search for Deeper Concerns

You may have already guessed our answer: Listen and communicate *openly* and *proactively*. Deeper concerns will naturally come out when you practice open and proactive communication. Again, the 10 strategies recommended in Chapter 7 concerning *how to listen more openly* apply here.

In addition to these 10 strategies, we have a few more specific suggestions for getting at deeper concerns. First, although we have cautioned against using "Why" questions, presented in an open and non-judgmental manner, they are useful for uncovering deep concerns. Our Mac thesaurus gives the following synonyms for "Why":

- How come?
- For what reason?
- For what purpose?
- What for?
- To what end?

Other more open-ended inquiries to consider:

- Tell me more.
- Can you explain that a little more?
- I don't understand what you mean exactly.

Our second suggestion is to meditate or contemplate on the surface issue, concern, or solution. How come you are so adamant about your surface concern? If the issue feels like a hot button for you, how come? What feelings and fantasies emerge as you contemplate the issue? Do other issues bring up similar feelings? How come?

For instance, when considering your insistence on a specific curfew time, you might discover that the general theme of letting go and releasing reappears over and over in different contexts in your life. Either individually or with the other person, write down the material that pops up as you

BRING OUT THE BEST IN OTHERS   103

search for deeper concerns.

One recurring issue that we have had in our marriage was Sheila not calling when she was going to get back late from work. Rick would worry about what was going on with her until she arrived home, and then, that anxiety would suddenly turn into anger. At that point, he was all anger, seemingly forgetting he had been worried about her a few moments earlier. We did not talk about the issue for a long time outside of the heat of the moment. When we finally did, we started making progress on the topic.

9

EXPECT THE BEST BUT DON'T BE CONTROLLED BY YOUR EXPECTATIONS

Expect the best

The Pygmalion effect

In the 1960s, Rosenthal and Jacobsen published research that supported *positive expectancy effects*, also known as the Pygmalion effect. In a paper written about 30 years after the initial studies, Rosenthal writes that he first got the idea to study expectancy effects when he realized he had serious problems in his dissertation data. In a December 1994 article published in *Current Directions in Psychological Science*, Rosenthal writes, "In the mid-1950s, the results of my doctoral dissertation were nearly ruined; it appeared that I might have treated my experimental subjects in such a way as to lead them to respond in accordance with my experimental hypothesis, or expectancy."[16]

To explore this possible expectancy effect, he followed up with maze learning studies in rats. Half the experimenters were told that their rats had been specially bred to learn mazes quickly while the other half were told their rats had been bred for poor maze learning. The experimenters with the "smarter" rats reported better learning from their subjects than the other group.

Rosenthal and Jacobsen then extended the experiments to grade school children. Kids in the first through sixth grades were given IQ tests. The researchers told the students' teachers that test results indicated that specific students (about 20 percent of the total students in their classes) would show remarkable gains in intellectual competence during the remainder of the school year. These "bloomers" had been randomly selected with no relationship to IQ test results. As Rosenthal writes, "The only difference between the experimental group and the control group children, then, was in the minds of the teachers." At the end of the school year, all the children were retested. "Overall, the children from whom the teachers had been led to expect greater intellectual gain showed a significantly greater gain than did the children of the control group, thereby supporting the 'Pygmalion' hypothesis."[17]

A limited number of studies have also studied the *Golem effect* or *negative expectations* of others. Generally, subjects have lived down to the negative expectations of others. However, there are obvious ethical problems in doing research designed to decrease subjects' performance, self-esteem, etc., so there are relatively few studies in this area.

Your reflections of positive expectations

Many people recall a teacher or other adult who was vitally important to their developing sense of self and their capabilities. Please spend a few moments right now recalling adults who affirmed your abilities and worth as a child or teen. Was there one adult who stands out in this regard? How did they demonstrate confidence in you? How did they convey positive expectations? How did this make you feel, and do you think it affected what you did?

Now, consider people to whom you have imparted positive expectations. How did you do this? Did you do this verbally? If so, was the message conveyed more by the content of what you said, how you said it, or both? Or did you express your expectations more by your body language or actions in some way? How did they respond? We hope you write down at least some of your thoughts and answers.

Your reflections of negative expectations

Think of people in your life who have shown negative expectations concerning you, as a child, adolescent, or adult. Again, who stands out? How did they show their negative expectations?

Lastly, think of people with whom you have had low or negative expectations. What was it about them, their circumstances, or their behavior that may have led you to these negative expectations? How did you demonstrate these expectations to them?

Of course, it is easier to demonstrate that you expect the best from people if you expect the best. However, assuming the best from people can be difficult at times. Although we will discuss this issue in a few moments, consider the above reflections a bit more. Below are some questions to guide you as you remember times you had negative expectations (or at least not positive expectations) of others.

- What was their gender, race, and age and did that affect your expectations?
- How did that person look? Did their appearance have any effect on your negative evaluation?
- Did this person remind you of someone else with whom you had difficulty? How did that influence your expectations?
- Was there a specific task or activity they were attempting (or might attempt), and you were concerned about their ability to complete it satisfactorily?
- If you knew the person reasonably well, what aspects of their history, life circumstances, prior behavior, and your interactions affected your expectations?
- Had you heard stories or other people's assessment of them that affected you?
- How were you generally feeling at the time you had the negative expectations? Was there anything about your current state that affected your judgment?
- How old were you when you had negative expectations toward the person? Do you think you would make the same judgment now? Why did you answer yes or no?
- Add your own questions.

Inborn prejudice

It is time to share the results of further research from Yale's Infant Cognition Center.[18] In Chapter 2 we described their research, which suggested that infants as young as three-months-old, showed a preference for a puppet who helped versus a puppet who obstructed another puppet.

In similar studies, they found infants prefer a puppet who more closely resembles themselves in some way. In one study, babies chose between two types of snacks, like Cheerios or graham crackers. The babies then see two animal puppets; one of the puppets likes Cheerios and rejects graham crackers while the other prefers graham crackers. Then, babies choose between the puppets. They usually picked the puppet who preferred the same snack the baby herself liked.

In the next part of the experiment, the puppet who chose the non-preferred snack (that the baby did not want) is trying to open a box. A second puppet helps while a third puppet tries to stop the other puppet from opening the box. Then, the babies are asked to choose between the helping or obstructing puppet. Almost 80 percent of babies under one-year-old chose the obstructing puppet while 100 percent of toddlers over one-year-old chose the obstructing puppet. The conclusion is that babies don't just want to help puppets similar to them but want to punish puppets that are dissimilar.

These findings suggest the tendency to associate with those more like us and reject those who are not like us has early developmental origins and is probably not just solely caused by our culture and incorporating our parents' or other significant adults' prejudices.

On some levels, it makes perfect sense that we have built-in programming that influences our identification with others based on perceived similarities. Few of us have a problem with infants and toddlers imitating other *humans* (as opposed to dogs and snakes) in learning to walk and talk among countless other skills and activities. Although infants may love their four-legged pets, they rarely continue to walk on their hands and legs as they develop. And many infants never bark at all. In other words, they want to be more like people than dogs. It is not a stretch to think that early on, they also discriminate between the less apparent differences of various races, genders, etc.

From our view, the point of these studies is that we all have inherent prejudices, which often take the form of liking those similar to us and either ignoring or disliking those who are different. This tendency may make it more difficult to have positive expectations towards people you perceive to be different from you. Some remedies for this follow.

Overcoming the obstacles toward positive expectations

Consider the following to help overcome the obstacles in expecting the best from others.

Go back to the above sections on *Your Reflections of Positive and Negative Expectations* to further explore aspects of others, yourself, and situations that may have influenced your positive or negative expectations of others in the past.

Bring your obstacles into consciousness. Many feelings, thoughts, and behavior are rooted in unconscious processes, which by definition, we are not consciously aware of. It is

difficult to change what we are not aware of. Meditate, contemplate, and pray about what might be blocking your ability
to expect the best from others. Remember that writing down
some of these revelations can help you see and work with
them in a different light. Recording these insights also enables
you to dig deeper and uncover more fundamental and firmly
rooted obstacles. Refer back to the section on unconscious
beliefs in Chapter 3 for an expanded discussion of these ideas
and strategies.

Look for similarities between yourself and others. As discussed earlier, research indicates that the more similar we see
ourselves to another person, the more favorably we tend to
view that person. Although all of us may be able to come up
with a few exceptions, is it so hard to believe that others are
human and want to be happy and avoid suffering, like you?

Another way to examine and change our negative reactions
to others is to do shadow work. Why do you have negative
thoughts and feelings toward specific people when others may
feel favorable or at least neutral toward those people? Please
see the 3-2-1 Shadow Process in Chapter 3 for details.

Don't be controlled by your expectations

Rick's mom would often say, "Don't get your hopes up too
high or you might be disappointed." You've probably heard
some version of this. Some years ago, our friend Tom seemed
to ignore this warning almost constantly and then suffer the
consequences. For instance, one morning he imagined going
to a local coffee shop with his wife. He visualized them sitting

at a table next to a window and watching the variety of people walking by. At this hour, he imagined there would be just a few others in the shop, and the place would be quiet, allowing he and his wife to take a well-deserved break from their busy and often hectic lives. He also imagined discussing their plans for an addition to their house, perhaps both of them using napkins to sketch out their ideas for the new family room. As it turned out, the place was unusually busy and noisy with no window tables available. The commotion made self-reflection difficult and communication between Tom and his wife impossible. And no napkins in sight. Tom was quickly overpowered by his disappointment, which soon turned to self-loathing and then anger at the world, including his wife. He walked out of the coffee shop without a word and returned home in the late afternoon to an unhappy spouse.

During our travels around Costa Rica and Panama during late 2016 and early 2017, we ran into many difficulties and unexpected situations, both of our own and others' making. For example, while walking on the beach in Montezuma, Sheila lost her treasured Bob Marley bandana. She had no idea when she lost it, but we decided to retrace our steps back down the beach. About 10 minutes later, we spotted a flag waving from a five-foot stick that had been stuck in the sand. It turned out to be the Marley bandana. Next to it, a guy was playing guitar near a tent. Soon, his female friend, who had found the bandana and made it into a flag for its owner to hopefully see, joined us. We listened to beautiful guitar music and talked together for an hour or so learning quite a bit about Montezuma and the couple.

We later realized that pretty much every time our plans had

gotten off-track, we would encounter unique, interesting, and often endearing people and situations that would never have happened without these detours.

So here are our thoughts about the dilemma To *Expect or Not to Expect*. Whenever doing anything, at least part of our motivation is that we are expecting some result. Whenever you go to the bathroom, are you not expecting a specific outcome—which will probably happen, but not always? Isn't that why you go in the first place? When you get in your car to go to the grocery store, aren't you expecting to buy specific things, bring them home, and then at some point consume them?

The problem is not with expecting specific results or outcomes. It seems inconceivable to live life without expectations. The *problem is investing so much emotional energy into particular expectations* so that when they are not met exactly, you melt down, become inflexible, and say, "If I can't have it exactly as I expect, I don't want anything at all." That way of thinking and feeling is just silly since hardly anything turns out precisely as you expect or picture it will.

The Bhagavad-Gita, a sacred Hindu text, says:

You have a right to your actions,
but never your actions' fruits.
Act for the action's sake ...

The wise man lets go of all
results, whether good or bad,
And is focused on the action alone.[19]

A more Western way of saying this is that we are responsible for what we do for our actions. The results are up to God. This certainly doesn't mean that we shouldn't closely observe and learn from the consequences of our actions. Also, the consequences of our previous actions should guide our future efforts. However, we shouldn't be too concerned if we did our best, and it didn't turn out quite the way we wanted or expected.

There is another NLP (neurolinguistic programming) saying that is pertinent here: *There is no failure, only feedback.* What this means to us is that most of the time, we do something to obtain a specific result. If our efforts don't produce the expected result, we have a choice of feeling we or others have failed or seeing these results as feedback, which can be used to change our future actions. So we can wallow in our failure, feel we don't or will never measure up, generally feel terrible about ourselves, and maybe even tell ourselves that we can never do anything right. Or we can see whatever response comes back from the universe as feedback that can be used to fine-tune our future actions.

Even when driving on a perfectly straight road, it's impossible to set the steering wheel and go forever. You will end up in the ditch or hitting a telephone pole. So you, mostly unconsciously, make fine adjustments with the steering wheel to stay on the road. Most of us don't start berating ourselves for not getting the steering wheel position "right" in the first place; we merely adjust as we go.

One of the problems with self-berating is that being so busy feeling upset with ourselves keeps us from paying close attention to what is actually happening. We don't learn from the experience and thus keep repeating the same mistakes over and over.

There is some truth in the statement that the most successful people have made the most mistakes. The surest way to never make a mistake is to never do anything at all. Of course, you won't get anything done or accomplished either, but at least, you won't be doing anything wrong.

It has been said that it took Thomas Edison 10,000 tries to get the electric lightbulb right. About halfway through his experiments, a friend said something like, "Tom, why don't you give up? You've tried 5,000 ways to get this to work, and you've learned nothing. It's all been a complete failure." Thomas replied, "I've learned a lot; now I know 5,000 ways not to do it."

Before moving on, we'd like to sum up and integrate the two ideas of expecting the best but not being controlled by expectations. This may seem contradictory at first glance.

Expectations are part of our human makeup and a crucial component in living. We would likely not do anything if we didn't expect something to happen as a result. However, investing large amounts of emotional energy into our expectations can result in blaming others, self-recrimination, and immobility when things are not working out as expected. Learn to use the outcomes of your actions as feedback to adjust your future behavior and not as self or other-berating opportunities.

When you attempt to bring out the best in others remember these three things:

- Your expectations of others' character and capabilities are significant and will influence your interactions with them and may have subtler effects.

- With practice, you will get better at bringing out the best in others, especially if you can observe what happens as neutrally as possible and learn from the experiences.

- Unlike some New Age thinking might imply, the results of your thoughts and actions are seldom solely up to you. The world does not revolve exclusively around you, your thoughts, and desires, at least from everyone else's point of view. This perspective urges us to take the results we get and creatively go with it. The ideal is to do our best with whatever is presented to us.

10

PACE BEFORE YOU LEAD

A motto from NLP that we especially like is to *Pace* before you *Lead*. In NLP, *pacing* means to join another person in some way by connecting with them in how they see the world or by mirroring or matching their external behavior, including characteristics of their speech and body posture and movement. *Pacing before leading* implies that establishing rapport with a person is the priority. Rapport is usually thought of as a two-way street, as a mutual understanding of each other's feelings, beliefs, and ideas. Rapport also requires being able to communicate this understanding with each other. However, this chapter focuses on inviting others to feel a connection *toward you*. Chapter 4 discusses in detail what you can do to feel a connection *toward others*.

Did you listen to Pope Francis's 2017 Ted Talk mentioned in our Introduction? Here is a short excerpt: "… I like when I hear parents talk to their babies, adapting to the little child, sharing the same level of communication. This is tenderness:

being on the same level as the other..."

Also, remember the seemingly inborn tendency to prefer those we find similar to us in some often superficial way. Humans show this tendency as young as three-months-old, and many of us continue in this tradition as adults.

The Pope's comments and the baby preference studies invite us to think about *pacing* as talking, acting, and appearing in ways so that others notice the similarities between you and them.

Before you can pace effectively, you need to observe others carefully. Since pacing is essentially matching various characteristics of others, you have to first carefully observe these aspects of the person, so you know what to match. We will discuss six primary considerations when pacing others:

- Search for and express what you have in common
- Demonstrate you understand their point of view
- Pace the content of their words
- Pace how you say things—variations in tone, pitch, loudness, phrasing, and speed
- Pace body language
- Pace appearance

Search for and express what you have in common

When you want others to notice similarities between you and them, search for what you have in common. You could start with carefully observing the person's appearance and how it in some way resembles yours. For people you have just met, notice their appearance, who is with them, what they are doing, and your mutual surroundings. Why is the weather such a popular topic of conversation? If you are anywhere near another person, you have the weather in common.

Pick a few similarities or things you resonate with concerning the other person and comment about it to them. For example, you might say, "I have shoes just like that. They're the most comfortable shoes I've ever worn."

Demonstrate you understand their point of view

Use the open listening skills detailed in Chapter 7 to explore their perspective on the topic you are discussing. Your sustained and nonjudgmental interest in their viewpoints will help develop their connection with you. Remember you don't have to express you agree with everything they say, just that you understand what they are saying.

Pace the content of their words

Chapter 6 examined what not to say, including malicious gossip. Below, we present two primary ways of deciding what to say to better pace and connect with others:

- Using Sensory Preferences
- Asking Questions

Using sensory preferences

In matching another person's content, it is often helpful to notice the words they use that indicate a specific sense—visual, auditory, or kinesthetic. Kinesthetic is the sense of feeling. Responding in the same sensory mode that they are using helps them feel more connected to you. For example, if they say, "It's *clear* to me that...", you might respond, "I *see* what you mean."

The following words and phrases represent specific senses. Listen to which group of words they are using at the moment and respond with a word from the same group as in the above example.

Visual Words: show, see, reveal, imagine, clear, appear, view, viewpoint, focus, picture, envision, foggy, bright, dim, look, dawn, short-sighted, long view, tunnel vision, paint a picture, bird's-eye view, illuminate, transparent, perceive, point out, observe, watch.

Auditory Words: hear, listen, rings a bell, harmonize, tuned in, tuned out, sounds right, note, resonates, voiced, loud and clear, on another note, tell, question.

Kinesthetic Words: feel, touch, hard, grasp, get ahold of, get a grip, throw out, catch on, follow, follow through, move, solid, firm grip, get in touch with, hang in there, pull some strings, tap into, sharp, dull, hand it to you, comfortable, uncomfortable.

Asking questions

Generally, people like to talk about themselves. You can assist by asking questions. Ask open-ended questions—those that require more than a yes or no response. For instance, instead of asking the person to tell you if they had a good day, ask them to tell you about their day. Your *intent* in asking questions is usually the most important aspect. Are you sincerely interested in what the person has to say, or are you primarily thinking or looking for a way to get your point across to them? This is explored more fully in Chapter 7, in the sections on open versus defensive communications. Remember that to form healthy and mutually satisfying connections with others, you need to be truly curious and interested in them.

Pace how you say things—variations in tone, pitch, loudness, phrasing, speed

While you are carefully listening to the content of what people are saying, also listen to how they are saying it. The phrase *tone of voice* refers to various speaking characteristics including variations in pitch, loudness, speed, and phrasing. Tone is a significant factor in conveying the emotional content of what is being said. Differences in these speech characteristics help determine the emotional content of the message.

According to a 2017 Internet article by Cheryl Posey, a licensed speech pathologist, a firm or harsh tone is achieved by controlling our voice so that changes in pitch within and between words are minimized, speaking volume is louder (we would add that important words are over-stressed), and facial expressions are more controlled with no smiling and perhaps some frowning.[20] A friendlier tone is achieved by making more pitch changes especially with stressed words and sometimes speaking at a lower volume. This usually sounds less aggressive although an excited voice may be loud. Ms. Posey adds that when we smile, our voice sounds more friendly and pleasing to others.

Ms. Posey also recommends an exercise to help us differentiate between different tones of voice. She recommends saying the sentences twice, once with a harsh, firm tone and once again with a friendly tone. You might also try interested versus uninterested tones or tones that imply belief versus non-belief in what you're saying. Consider recording and closely listening to your sentences. Below is a sample of sentences inspired by her article.

- Good morning.
- What you said sounds logical.
- It's great to see you again.
- See you later. Have a good day.

Exercise

Focus on the emotional tone when listening to others. You might start with TV shows or movies in a language you don't know, so you can better focus just on the emotional tone and not the content of the words. You might start with just listening and not looking at the screen, so you can focus on the sound. Also, by practicing with a TV show or video, instead of an actual person in front of you, you are more likely to just listen instead of preparing what you are going to say back.

After you're comfortable with the above exercise, listen carefully to the tone of others when engaged in routine conversations. A Word of Caution: When you are listening to the voice tone of others, remember that the person's voice tone may or may not have anything to do with you, what you might have said, or the current situation. All of us carry around emotional baggage from other parts of our lives and sometimes dump them wherever we happen to be at the moment.

Pacing emotional tone

As said before, it is essential to establish a connection with others by pacing them in some way before sharing your feelings, viewpoint, beliefs, etc. Emotional pacing involves reflecting one or more aspects of the other's emotional tone. However, trying to mirror all aspects of the other person's emotional tone is not necessary and may be insulting to them.

Instead, choose one or two qualities of their emotional tone and then match them, more or less. For example, the person may be upset and demonstrates this by talking quickly with a loud volume and little variation in pitch. He doesn't even appear to crack a smile. The person will likely not feel much connection with you if you respond to him in an exceptionally calm and cheerful manner by talking softly and slowly while beaming at the person.

On the other hand, if you try to mimic them as accurately as possible, they will probably feel you are—well, trying to mimic them. Again, this doesn't usually lead to an enhanced feeling of connection. Instead, respond with one or two aspects of their emotional tone. In this case, you might try to match their speed of talking and raise your volume somewhat, not trying to match their speed and volume precisely.

Pace Body Language

Our emotional tone is suggested by our body language in addition to the verbal cues and facial expressions discussed above. It is generally thought that crossing the arms and displaying a stiff posture relate a closed and defensive mindset while a more relaxed posture and open hands suggest an open and inclusive attitude. Open hands also indicate that you have nothing to hide. A friendly smile is a universal sign that you come in peace.

In addition to sensibly applying some universal body signals, pay close attention to the person's posture and other body language characteristics. Then, more or less mirror one or two aspects of their body language to more fully connect with them. This can be fairly subtle. For example, if they are tapping their foot at a specific pace, you could more obviously tap your foot the same way. But to be more delicate about it, you could tap your index finger at about the same speed on the arm of a chair or your thigh.

Adjust your appearance

While working on getting residency status in Panama, our lawyer repeatedly told us to wear long pants, shirts with sleeves, and shoes that covered the feet (no shorts, sleeveless shirts, or sandals) when going to governmental agencies. The process at each agency went quickly and smoothly, partly due to our lawyer's expertise, but also to our complying with basic cultural expectations—mostly by dressing appropriately.

Although you may not be able to change what you are wearing at the moment in order to match (to some degree) those with whom you want to bring out their best, it's easier than trying to change other aspects of your appearance, such as height, weight, skin color, facial characteristics, etc. You might counter differences in height by kneeling when talking to a child so your eyes are approximately level with each other. Just use some common sense with your apparel—to more or less match others in the culture or situation you are in.

———————

Sometimes you need to *fit in,* but at other times you might want to *stand out.* Several years ago, our daughter, Sara, spent a year teaching English to children in Seoul, South Korea. About five feet, nine inches tall, she soon realized she stood out with her differences in height and skin color. She grew to enjoy the attention (almost always pleasant and appropriate) she received from her appearance. Upon returning to Lawrence, Kansas, she felt somewhat unnoticed, unappreciated, and sad as she fit in so perfectly.

11

―᷐᷐―

OTHER SPECIFIC
STRATEGIES, PART 1

Be 100 percent there
(at least part of the time)

How do you feel when you are talking with someone who appears to be giving about half of their attention to the conversation? Think about this for a few moments. What is going on that makes you suspect they are not giving the conversation their full attention?

They may be:

- Not looking at you much
- Engaged in some other activity such as looking at their cell phone
- Responding to your questions or comments in seem-

ingly non-related ways
- Appearing to fall asleep or looking bored
- Responding before you have finished your question or comment

You can't always stop everything you are doing whenever someone says something to you. You probably don't have time for a long discussion every time your child asks a question or makes a comment. However, if you want your relationships to grow (most long-term relationships either grow or self-implode), giving the person your full attention, at least at times, is critically important.

For a few moments, remember times when others have given you their full attention. For now, think of one-to-one encounters where the person is giving you positive attention. What did they do to make you feel they were giving you their full attention? How did you feel in response to their attention?

How do you show someone you are giving them 100 percent of your attention?

- Look at them often. You don't have to stare into their eyes for minutes at a time (that would just be weird), but do engage in some eye contact. We have heard of some research that concluded 20-second continuous eye contact is the upper limit, but as little as three-seconds at a time works pretty well.
- Give an occasional nod or uh huh to signal you are following what they are saying.
- Be aware of your overall body language. Leaning forward signals interest. It's usually good to keep your eyes open. Research indicates our pupils enlarge when

we see something that interests us although you probably don't have much voluntary control over this.

- Notice what you appreciate about them—how they look, how they present themselves, what they say, how they say it, etc.
- Don't do much else. Okay, if you have an itch, scratch it (depending on where the itch is and whom you are with).
- Don't interrupt; wait until they are done with their comments or question before you reply.
- Listen as much as possible before considering your reply.
- Your response should have something to do with their comment or question.

Expand your comfort zone

All of us have a comfort zone—a range of *behaviors* and *situations* where we feel calm, relaxed, and comfortable. Two processes naturally occur which tend to increase our comfort zone:

- We get more skillful and competent in numerous aspects of life.
- Our worldview generally expands as we gain experience and mature.

It is often a good idea to steer away from situations and behaviors where we are not competent. For example, flying a Boeing 747 is outside our comfort zone. Free climbing 1000 foot sheer cliffs is also outside our comfort zone. It's healthy for both of us, and in the first case, also for others that we don't engage in these behaviors. Although paying attention to and going along with your comfort zone can keep you alive, it can also unnecessarily restrict your life.

How do the restricting aspects of our comfort zone develop? The short story is that as babies, being liked and loved by others is necessary for our survival. We are completely helpless for an extended time after birth. Our pleasure of bonding with others, usually our mother, along with our horror of possible rejection may be a necessary element in our survival as babies. However, the remnant of the horror of rejection often stays with us long past the point of its usefulness in our physical survival. As adults, we likely avoid engaging in certain situations and behaviors because even thinking about them brings out uncomfortable feelings, including the fear of looking silly or stupid and often tied to the fear of rejection.

The first step to reaching outside your comfort zone is to realize that the disapproval, rejection, and criticism of others is unlikely to be fatal. You can live through being made fun of, being teased and even the strong condemnation by others.

The second step is to get more competent in whatever you'd like to do that right now feels outside your comfort zone. Practicing any of the mental or behavioral exercises in this book will help you become more competent in bringing out the best in others and will naturally extend your comfort zone.

The third step is to start taking "baby steps" in your exterior world—trying out new behaviors or old behaviors in new situations. This is sometimes called *shaping* behavior. Decades ago, Rick's graduate assistant duties included running experiments with mice and rats. One set of experiments involved observing how various reinforcement schedules affected a specific behavior, often the frequency of pressing a bar. However, if we had waited for the mouse to press the bar for the first time to get the pellet of food, we would have been waiting a very long time. Therefore, we would shape this behavior by at first reinforcing them for just turning in the direction of the bar, later for moving in that direction, and then for raising one of their front legs. In other words, we reinforced the small steps necessary for bar pressing.

You can essentially do the same thing. If one of your goals is to be able to relate to others in small groups of strangers, perhaps groups of 10 or so, you can start by talking with one person you know fairly well. Over time, you can gradually expand your comfort zone by talking with several people at a time and with people you don't know so well. You can slowly work up to relating to 10 or more people whom you have just met.

It is often helpful to write down the "baby steps" you need to take to reach a particular goal. Although you can brainstorm and write down the steps in any order, you should then reorder the list starting with the action that feels most within your current comfort zone. Then, move on to the step that stretches you just a bit more, and so on, until the last item on the list represents the action that feels most outside your comfort zone right now.

Writing down this behavioral list, from most comfortable to least comfortable, with the intention of gradually enacting each item, can be thought of as a type of goal setting which can be an extremely powerful tool in acquiring new behaviors and functioning well in new situations.

You can also combine this hierarchical approach with the

Mental Rehearsal and *Stealing Behavior* strategies discussed in Chapter 3. You may often feel competent and comfortable performing a specific behavior in a particular situation but not in other circumstances. In this case, you can start with third-person (like you are observing yourself as an actor in a movie) and then first-person (like you are seeing the scene out of your own eyes and you are the actor) mental movies of performing this behavior in comfortable circumstances and gradually change the elements of the situation so that you eventually see yourself implementing the action in what had been the least comfortable situations for you.

The baby-steps approach is generally synonymous with psychotherapy's systematic desensitization, which aims to cope with fear and anxiety. This approach is also useful in helping us gradually acquire the skills necessary to handle more and more complex situations successfully. Another way to approach new situations, if you already have the basic skills, is to jump right into the thick of things. In the psychological literature, this is called flooding.

The beginning of this section listed that a second way of naturally increasing our comfort zone occurs as we expand our worldview through experience and maturing. Being familiar with basic developmental concepts can expand our worldview, enlarge our comfort zone, and increase empathy and tolerance toward others. Although outside the scope of this book, we encourage you to explore various theories of human development, including Jean Piaget's cognitive development, Erik Erikson's psychosocial stages, Lawrence Kohlberg's moral development, and James Fowler's faith development theories. Ken Wilber describes numerous theories of human development in many of his books. Wilber's book, *Integral Psychology*, provides a comprehensive introduction to development while comparing over 100 theories of development.

A meditation, contemplation, or prayer practice can also move us forward in several areas of development.

Be bold

Bold individuals are willing to take risks, to do things that are outside of their comfort zone, and speak and act in ways that might be considered outside the mainstream. Keep in mind, we are not talking about being bold when you are concerned with your physical safety.

Think back to a time when you wanted to swim in a pool, lake, or ocean that felt rather cold when you first dipped your toes into it. Assuming you didn't turn and walk away, how did you approach getting into the water? Rick tends to use the baby steps method, putting in the toes of his right foot and then the whole foot, followed by the toes of his left foot, the entire left foot, and then gradually inching his legs further into the water. He often stops at the top of his thighs to renew his strength and resolve to continue this gradual process with the upper half of his body. In contrast, Sheila tends to jump or dive in. Once you plunge, there is no turning back, for better or worse. Sheila's method provides a more intense shock to the system, but the shock is resolved quickly. Rick's strategy gives a series of less intense shocks, which goes on for several minutes or more.

Being **bold** seems more like diving into the water. When you jump head-on into an unfamiliar situation that is outside your comfort zone, your anxiety often dissipates relatively quickly. Anxiety often occurs when we are *thinking* about doing something we imagine will be uncomfortable. However, by jumping into the situation and taking action, anxiety often decreases or even vanishes. When we can be fully in the current situation and take action at the present moment, there is little room left to worry about what might happen next.

If you are still doubtful of your ability to be bold and act in the face of fear, read *Feel The Fear And Do It Anyway* by Susan Jeffers.

Dare to be different

Sometimes you have to say or do things differently from others for people to notice and engage with you. When we first meet someone at a social gathering, the usual process is to exchange names and then ask the typical questions concerning where they are from, where they live now, and what they do, usually regarding making an income. Questions can then get more personal, asking about their marital status, if they have children, and how they came to be at this gathering. All of that is fine, but it doesn't create much momentum to establish a deeper relationship. In his book, *Connect with Anyone: How to Be Instantly Likable, Irresistibly Charming, and Quickly Connect with People On a Deep Level*, Dominic Mann promotes asking unusual questions that surprise the other person and calls for more in-depth reflection than the usual questions given above.[21] He recommends the following types of questions:

- How would you rate the meaningfulness of your life on a scale of zero to ten?

- What's the most embarrassing thing that's ever happened to you?
- What is one thing you've always wanted to do but never did? Why haven't you done it?
- Where would you go if you could go anywhere?
- What do you value most in life?
- Tell me the most embarrassing thing you've ever done.
- If you knew you'd be dead tomorrow, what would you do today?

Mann relates that at a talent show, he sat down next to a woman he had never seen before. Instead of small talk, the first thing he said to her was, "So, what's your favorite thing about life?" Reportedly, this was the beginning of a passionate relationship, which was still continuing during the time he wrote the book.

Give consistent messages by matching the content and delivery of your message

The *content* of a message is provided by the words and how they are arranged. This is what we get when reading something.

The *auditory delivery* of the message includes the *tone* and *inflection* the speaker uses. Inflection is essentially a change in tone. A declarative statement such as, "You are leaving today," can be made into a question by raising the pitch of your voice when you work up to the word "today." We get this added component when talking with someone over the phone.

The *visual delivery* of a message involves our body language, including facial expression. We gain this added dimension when speaking with someone face-to-face. Although this tone of the message comes through best when we are actually with the person, a watered-down version can be obtained by using Skype or FaceTime.

You have probably heard that the impact of a spoken message is around 10 percent verbal (content) and 90 percent nonverbal (auditory and visual delivery). This comes from Albert Mehrabian's research from the late 1960s.[22] However, this applies only to emotionally laden messages where content and delivery do not match. For instance, it usually doesn't apply when you are explaining a formula in quantum physics where the content provides the main message whether you are excited about it or not.

The primary take away from Mehrabian's research is that when you are expressing an emotionally laden message and the *content* of your words do not match your *delivery*, most people will determine the meaning from the delivery, not the content of the words. Imagine you ask someone how they are doing, and they respond, "I feel great" while slumping forward, head and eyes lowered as they mutter the words quietly and almost unintelligibly with a monotone voice. Are you likely to think they are really feeling great?

However, fully expressing hurt and anger to others doesn't usually work well. Most of us get defensive when someone directs their deep hurt and anger at us.

If you want to discuss something that you are furious about at the moment, we recommend waiting until both you and the other person are relatively calm. You can still talk about the intensity of your feelings, but talking about it in the past tense usually allows the other person to listen less defensively. You can also still be congruent in emphasizing the seriousness of the matter.

Ideally, when initiating discussions where there is an underlying conflict, start with centering yourself with feelings of love and caring, being ready to listen openly to the other person's point of view, and having a general attitude of trying to work things out, while giving up the stance of blaming the other person for everything.

Use "I" messages

The primary functions of I-messages are to take responsibility for your feelings, reduce defensive reactions from the person you are talking with, and open the door to discuss the issue and possible solutions with them.

Instead of saying, "You make me feel afraid and angry when you don't call and let me know that you will be home late," you might say, "I feel afraid and angry when you're not home on time, and I don't know why you are not home."

In the latter statement, you are expressing how you feel and connecting those feelings to the other person's behavior, at least indirectly. Although you are not charging the person for *making* you feel a certain way, you are implying their role in it. The final part of the I-statement is to ask them what they think and feel about what you have said or expressing that you would like to talk more about this.

Here is what we consider an optimal formula for I-messages...

1. State your feelings and take responsibility for them—do not blame the person by saying they "made you feel" a certain way.
2. Connect your feelings directly or indirectly with the other person's actions.
3. Invite the other person to dialogue with you about the issue with the intent of both understanding each other better and coming up with a trial solution.

I feel _____ when you _____. Could we talk about this? or What are you thinking about this?

The person may still feel you are blaming them and get defensive. Of course, you *are* blaming them; if they had acted differently, you would not be feeling this way.

Remember this: the *way* you say it, or your emotional tone, will likely have more to do with the other person's reaction than the content of your words. Please see the final section of Chapter 12 for another take on this strategy.

Apologize

In the above discussion, *I-messages* are recommended when expressing what you don't like about another's behavior. Of course, it is would be also great to use I-messages when thanking others for what they have done. Your remarks could be modeled after the first sentence of the I-message formula. You probably don't need to add the second sentence in asking what the person thinks about your comment or suggesting that you discuss it further.

However, there is a completely different situation where the first phrase of the I-Message Formula should be applied. That situation is when you feel the need to apologize to someone for your own actions that may have negatively impacted them, in other words, when you think you have hurt them.

Most of us are experts at being offended or wounded by what others say or do. Perhaps neuroscientists will someday discover two fault finding centers in the brain. If they do, the center for finding fault in others will likely be enormous compared to the microscopic self-fault finding center.

This is to say that it is difficult for many of us to *even recognize* that we may have said or done something that harms others. And if we do recognize that possibility, we are usually quick to blame others for our actions. Our thoughts and verbal explanations often echo the childhood refrain, "They started it."

Think about this. Is it likely that you can bring out the best in someone who feels anger and resentment toward you? Our answer... probably not.

The eighth and ninth steps in Alcoholics Anonymous are listed below.

8. We made a list of all persons we had harmed, and became willing to make amends to them all.
9. We made direct amends to such people wherever possible, except when to do so would injure them or others.

Step 8 asks one to consider everyone we might have harmed while step 9 essentially asks us to refine that list to persons for whom it would be practically possible and not harmful for us to approach directly.

But how do you know that you have harmed someone? We know several people who appear to be kind and loving toward everyone they meet, yet they post unkind and potentially hurtful comments on social media. These comments often target large groups of people they don't agree with. In some cases, it is possible that these usually kind people don't realize or consider the impact their comments may have on those reading it. Or maybe they rationalize they are just standing up for what they believe. We don't know.

Our point is that with the internet and social media, our opportunity to hurt others has greatly expanded. When you post a comment on Facebook or Twitter, you will likely not get any feedback from the majority of people you have upset. In addition, any feedback you get is seldom immediate. In short, the opportunities for one to experience the consequences of their social media and other internet actions is minimized and take a different form from what we are used to. Our ability to detect and correct our behavior is diminished.

Even when interacting with someone on a one-to-one basis, the other person may not clearly communicate that what you have said or done has been hurtful to them. Perhaps the best we can do is to attune our empathy and sensitivity toward others as much as possible. If you receive any signals that you might have hurt or upset the person, straightforwardly ask about this.

Some may argue that upsetting another person might, in certain situations, be the only way to eventually bring out their best. This can get complicated quickly. Specific behaviors that are acceptable according to one person's moral, religious, and political beliefs may be grave sins for another.

Given all the complexities of this issue, our recommendation is to start with situations where you know you have harmed another person. You can start with the first phrase of the I-Message Formula and say something like, "I feel terrible and am sorry that I ..."

In most cases, it is best to stop talking and give ample time for the other person to respond. Don't be impatient. Let them respond on their own time. This is not the time to explain why you did what you did.

Be aware that the person might respond defensively, which will probably feel like they are attacking you. Not jumping in to defend yourself is often extremely difficult for most of us. Do your best to listen openly to them. Try to limit your responses to reflecting back what they have said in the spirit of trying to better understand their thoughts and feelings. Again, this is not easy. If it is helpful, you might see this as part of your repentance for your prior behavior.

Note: You can access much information concerning AA's steps 8 and 9 on the internet. We found the following sites helpful.

- https://www.evergreendrugrehab.com/blog/step-8-9-work-making-amends-meaning/
- https://www.aa.org/assets/en_US/en_step8.pdf
- https://www.aa.org/assets/en_US/en_step9.pdf

You can also Google "AA steps 8 and 9" or "making amends aa."

12

OTHER SPECIFIC STRATEGIES, PART 2

Share others' interests and expand Your own

You can share an interest in learning about someone's passion for something even if you don't share the same passion. This idea is from Dominic Mann's book referenced in Chapter 11. Although it appeared to be a simple suggestion, it seemed profound to us. In Mann's own words, "Your job isn't to be passionate about everything. Your job is to identify what somebody is passionate about, and then talk to them about it. That's it."[23] Even if you're not passionate about something, you can still be interested in it. Can you be interested in someone else's passion for at least a few minutes without being passionate about it yourself?

Mann also discourages faking passion or liking. He adds,

"Don't pretend to like things that you don't. However, there's a big difference between 'liking' something and being 'interested' in something."[24]

Expand your range of interests

In their book, *People Skills at Work*, Evan and Dira Berman write:

> People who make many connections often have a wide range of interests. They read up on many subjects and engage with others in small talk in which these interests are explored. We don't always know what we will find interesting, and it is useful to be open to the interests and hobbies of others.[25]

So how do we expand our range of interests? There is a reciprocal relationship between making connections with others and developing a wide range of interests. As you develop a wider range of interests, it is easier to connect with others, and as you connect with others, you will naturally expand your range of interests. Of course, you've got to talk with others about their and your interests.

Chapter 7 offered the image of being an explorer in new territory as an analogy of exploring the beliefs and interests of others. One point of the analogy is that you can better learn about others when you suspend judgment and treat your encounters with the spirit of discovery instead of critical analysis.

Parents often encourage their kids to try new things, like new foods or activities. "You won't know if you'll like it until you try it." So try a lot of new things. However, remember we also often talk about *acquired* tastes, which means that you have to try some things a number of times before you start to like them. The online Urban Dictionary gives the example of the music of Frank Zappa as an acquired taste. If you only pursue what you immediately enjoy, you will probably keep your interests in a narrow range.

Sheila was a fine arts major in college. My areas of focus were drawing and ceramics. I loved drawing and spent years working with different mediums but using only black and white and shades of gray. This felt very comfortable.

I disliked a required course in oil painting because the use of color was mandatory. I was intimidated by using color. Although I grudgingly completed the requirements, I avoided working in color after the class ended, going back to my black, gray, and white world.

About 10 years later, I took a watercolor class and found enjoyment in learning to use color. This spurred me on to explore other ways to use color in art. Now, I always use color in my artwork.

Soft eyes

They teach the concept of soft eyes or soft focus in martial arts. The idea is to use a relaxed, wide, peripheral focus as opposed to a tense, narrow, central focus. Again, the idea is to observe, not judge. It's like being able to see the forest and the trees at the same time. Martial artists practice this to fend off attacks from all directions.

You can practice soft eyes right now. Although some say soft eyes is done a bit like crossing your eyes, we think it is the opposite of this. Hold the palm of one hand four to six inches directly in front of your eyes and focus on the center of your palm. Then, move your palm to one side and focus on something four to five feet away without moving your eyes up or down or to one side or the other. Do this several times while observing how your eyes converge when looking at your palm and diverge when looking further away. Then, try to diverge the eyes just a bit more to expand your peripheral vision. You can also practice attending more to your peripheral awareness.

You can apply *soft eyes* to developing interests in both a literal, external way and a metaphorical, inner way. The first way is to literally look at what is interesting to you with the soft eyes technique described above. This can help you see background and context to your object of interest. You can also use *soft eyes* as a metaphor for exploring your mind. Instead of focusing narrowly on one topic or interest, let your mind, including your thoughts and imagination, widen to include the broader context.

Drive yourself to distraction

Many authors comment that persons with ADHD are more creative than others, and there is some research to back up this statement. In his clinical practice, Rick would often tell parents of ADHD kids that, in a sense, you have to be distracted to be creative.

The stereotypical ADHD person will say a sentence or two about a topic or idea, which will lead to another idea, which will lead to another idea, and so on and on. We often do this when daydreaming or brainstorming. Do this occasionally, just letting your mind wander. If you want to do this more formally, use a mind map, which visually organizes pieces of information (including ideas, people, places, and things) according to interrelationships. Go to https://en.wikipedia.org/wiki/Mind_map for more details on this.

A journal article by Darya L. Zabelina and Michael D. Robinson describes the effects of asking adults to imagine they were seven-years-old as they completed a writing task.[26] They found these subjects expressed more creative originality in their writing than subjects who were not told to visualize they were seven-years-old. So, if you want to think outside-the-box, imagine you think like you did when you were seven. Incidentally, the authors mention that one reason adults seem to show less creative originality than children is that "creativity... *may* be stifled by the educational system."

By the way, we found Darya and Michael's article by first Googling "mind map," which led us to a resource, which led us to another resource, which led us to yet another and then to Darya and Michael's article. Serial Googling is a high-tech way to let your mind wander.

Write a letter

Our youngest daughter, Sara, told us about a specific strategy she has used that she believes helps bring out the best in others in a long-lasting way. In her own words:

My 23rd birthday sticks out to me for a couple of reasons. I was in grad school that year, living in a new town, and I was trying to host a little birthday gathering for myself. I missed the years prior where there was someone around to throw the party for me and take care of all the details. I felt a little strange that I was hosting this party for myself, and I remember tearfully calling my parents the day before as I felt a bit worried that my new friends wouldn't come and a bit bummed that I would be baking myself a birthday cake. Well, many friends came through (and so did my parents, secretly ordering me a fancy bakery cake for the party), but that wasn't the only reason this birthday goes down in the books.

Another reason was that I received quite a few cards from my friends that year. But some of these cards were different from the ones I usually received for birthdays. This year, many of my friends wrote long messages and identified the characteristics they appreciated in me. I had received meaningful, personalized messages such as these from my parents, sister and best friend, but not from people that I was beginning new friendships with. I was touched by their words, and I still have those cards to this day. I realized that these written gestures grasped me in a way that was different than if they had been said.

When that school year ended, I graduated, wrapped up an AmeriCorps placement I was involved in, and said goodbye to the friends I had made because I was on my way to South Korea for a year. I decided to write a card to each person I had worked with at my placement as well as several amazing professors and friends I had made during graduate school. I spent hours on this and made a point to write them similarly to the birthday cards I had received.

When writing them, I skipped over the more generic statements and instead reflected on the specific things I had learned from the person and the qualities and characteristics I appreciated and admired—I was highlighting what I saw as *being the best in these people.*

After my year of teaching English in Korea, I also wrote

cards to each student I taught and each significant person I had encountered that year. Again, it took me hours to do this, but I am so glad I did. It gave me closure in these goodbyes. And it touched the people who had been so important to me. My meditation instructor in South Korea told me that he had never received a letter so meaningful and thoughtful. Several others gave me feedback of utmost appreciation for the letters/cards.

And I ended up benefiting even more from ways I couldn't imagine at the time. I returned to Lawrence, Kansas, after my year in Korea and inquired about getting a job where I did my Americorps practicum. It turned out that someone I had worked with and written a card to had become the team leader of the team I wanted to join.

After he hired me, he told me (on my first day of work) that he still had that card. He added that he had been so touched by it that he took a picture of it and sent it to his wife.

I also wrote a card for a rather delightful and handsome friend I met in Lawrence before my year in Korea. When I returned, I learned he kept that card with him in his backpack all year. We have been happily dating for several years. Of course, I am not saying that writing these letters was the only factor that landed me my current job and boyfriend, but I sure don't think they hurt!

My point is that a good way to bring out the best in people is to reflect on what is the best in them in your eyes and let them know in writing! Telling them is an excellent way to communicate this, but there is something different about a letter. It takes time, and it is something that person can hold and read time and again.

Laugh at yourself & situations

Although the *Joy* chapter briefly discussed seeing the humor in yourself and situations, this idea is expanded on here because we believe this is an extremely important skill to develop—for both your exterior and interior worlds.

Sheila has always enjoyed and been thankful for a good sense of humor. It has helped me to remain more optimistic and fun loving during calm and relatively normal periods of life. However, during some exceptionally bleak days and months in the past, I came to treasure its blessings. During the darker days, I felt it was a mark of progress to make or laugh at a joke between crying jags. Circumstances required finding dark humor in the absurdity of our extreme situation. Gallows humor has its place and can help us move into more acceptance of our sufferings and perhaps provide a bit of relief as we become more able to shift focus with a wider view. Having outside sources (friends, relatives, YouTube videos, etc.) to provide this type of humor is invaluable when our own well is dry. There were times when my nephew's creative, quick-witted, and rather wicked sense of humor turned the gloom into laughter.

As I was growing up, I used sarcasm as the primary tool of humor, finding mirth in putting down people, including their appearance and behavior. I became an expert but did not realize how painful this could be for others since I was focused on how funny and clever I was being. When I was about 16-years-old, I laid out heavy sarcasm in conversing with my mother. When she stopped laughing, she said, "That's so funny, but you are *vicious*!"

I felt instant shock when I realized I was hurting people even as they laughed and that I needed to find other styles of humor instead. I did not want to be vicious. Initially, I turned to self-depreciating humor, which removed other people from the bull's eye. I still frequently use self-depreciating jokes as I generally accept myself and my shortcomings, and it seems to provide me with unending source material!

In *The Book of Joy*, Douglas Abrams remarked, "I once heard that laughter was the most direct line between any two people, and certainly the Dalai Lama and Archbishop Tutu use humor to break down the social barriers that separate us."[27] Archbishop Tutu recounts how he used humor in dealing with volatile situations, including funerals for those killed by the police in South Africa:

> People were really angry and you'd have the police standing not far away—and it was an explosive situation. Anything could have gone wrong. My weaponry, if you can call it that, was almost always to use humor, and especially self-denigrating humor, where you are laughing at yourself.[28]

Both Archbishop Tutu and the Dalai Lama add specific stories of how they used humor in horrific circumstances. Although we have said it before, we urge you to get a copy of *The Book of Joy* and immerse yourself in it.

Effects of Laughter and Humor

Research has shown that humor can bolster our immune system and cardiac functioning; decrease stress, anxiety, pain, and anger; and increase positive mood.

Although there is a fair amount of research pointing to the benefits of laughter and using humor for our well-being, humor is unlikely to ever to get the Gold Standard Stamp of Approval from the medical community. It can't be capsuled or bottled up like medication and used in a double-blind placebo study. (More cynically, you can't bottle up humor and sell it at ridiculous prices.)

A double-blind study assures that neither the subjects nor the experimenters administering the treatment (the independent variables) and assessing the effects (changes in the dependent variables) know if the person is consuming the actual treatment (often medication) or is taking a placebo. A placebo looks like, feels like, and tastes like the real thing. It's hard to imagine how you would make and apply a humor placebo.

Although it is not scientific research, Norman Cousins's story provides inspiration for those wanting to add more humor in their lives. In 1964, Cousins, who had been a long-time editor of *Saturday Review*, developed a rare disease of the connective tissues, Ankylosing Spondylitis. He was told he had a few months to live. Since the medical community offered him no hope, he came up with his own plan. Knowing that negative emotions can often lead to physical problems, Cousins decided to barrage himself with positive emotions—primarily with laughter. Allen Funt, the producer of *Candid Camera,* sent films of some of his classic shows along with a movie projector. They also found old Marx Brothers films.

In his book, *Anatomy of an Illness*, Cousins writes, "It worked. I made the joyous discovery that 10 minutes of genuine belly laughter had an anesthetic effect and would give me at least two hours of pain-free sleep."[29] The only side effect was that his movies were disturbing other patients in the hospital. He moved into a nearby hotel to continue his self-designed therapy while making continual progress. Instead of a few months, he lived another 26 years.

Developing your sense of humor

The following provides some strategies to get you started developing your funny bone—both appreciating various forms of humor and learning to be humorous to others.

Listen to audio and watch TV and internet videos that promise to be humorous. (Think of Norman Cousins watching Marx Brothers movies to cure himself.) Look for comedy shows on TV and Netflix, google "stand-up comedians" on Youtube, and search the internet. Note one caution here. There are a number of comedy shows and stand-up comedians who use extreme, rough, and insulting humor. The people who pay to be insulted by these artists usually know what they are getting into. It is up to you to discern whether a specific joke is appropriate in a specific situation. Carefully observing the feedback you get from others will tell you a lot.

Check out from the library or buy humorous books or magazines. We used to love parts of *Mad Magazine*. Try out Laughter On Line University (http://www.laughteronlineuniversity.com/) or other humor sites on the internet.

Whenever you find yourself laughing, notice what it is that seems funny to you. Was it more about the absurdity of the situation or did the person delivering the humor do an exceptional job; if so, how did they do it?

Learn to laugh at yourself. Laughing at yourself is a great way to use humor in difficult situations and connect with others. It usually conveys a sense of humbleness. It helps to open up communication between yourself and others. Gentle self-depreciatory humor can also be useful because others will rarely knock down another if the other person is already knocking down him or herself.

Acquaint yourself with various types of humor. This will expand your thinking about it and allow you to see the potential for humor in more areas of life. Googling *Types of Humor* found articles categorizing humor into three to 20 types. For now, we will briefly discuss four types.

- **Positive humor** emphasizes the contradictions and absurdities in situations and life in general. Often, the punch line can deliver an unexpected and enjoyable surprise. This type of humor often leads to a more affiliative atmosphere among people.
- **Negative humor** often targets oneself or others in a demeaning way. Think of blonde jokes and Polish jokes, which may be hilarious unless you are blonde and Polish.
- **Teasing humor** gently makes fun of yours or another's beliefs, attitudes, behavior, or appearance. Explore *The Book of Joy* for examples of how two old men with widely different surface beliefs can enhance their love and enjoyment of each other with good-natured teasing.
- **Distraction humor** pulls us away from grim or uncomfortable realities. This type of humor may serve well as a momentary reprieve and smooth over negative feelings and interactions but may also serve to avoid recurrent areas of concern that are best dealt with seriously.

The two most important strategies

We have covered many strategies in these past six chapters. However, we want to point out the two that are especially important and may at times override others. Those two strategies are to practice open listening and to be proactive. The proactive strategy applies mostly to ongoing relationships.

Bringing out the best in ourselves and others is always a work in progress. Sheila and Rick are still working to bring out the best in each other more consistently. During the two years of writing and rewriting this book, one or the other of us has occasionally said, "Maybe we should be practicing what we are saying in the book."

Another point stems from a conversation we had while walking down the streets of El Valle a few months ago. The discussion involved how we could do better at not reactively pressing each other's hot buttons on certain topics. Sheila had pointed out earlier that it was the anniversary of our first date, 30-plus-years-ago. In the interim, we had rarely squandered the countless opportunities to push those buttons. Semi-joking aside, although we have made a lot of progress, our efforts to improve in these areas are ongoing.

Getting back to our conversation, we specifically talked about how to state our concerns using the I-message formula described in Chapter 11. Remember that our version of the I-Message Formula includes stating your feelings, connecting those feelings to the other person's actions, and then inviting them to discuss it. The formula is: *I feel* _____ *when you*_____. *Could we talk about this?* Or *What do you think about this?*

During that early August discussion, we mutually decided that the above formula often led to a defensive reaction in the other person. After more discussion, we agreed that when one of us was upset, that person would simply state their feelings and not connect it to any specific causes. The other person would do their best to listen openly, to explore the other's thoughts and feelings, and to inquire about the connections to our partner's emotions, including its perceived causes. That person could then talk about their own thoughts concerning the situation, and we could discuss possible solutions together.

We recommend that in an ongoing relationship you proactively discuss communication strategies and tweak them as appropriate, especially when they have not been working so well. You might mutually decide some need specific adjustments and that others don't work for the two of you. You might devise completely different strategies to try.

Our basic approach could be summed up: Practice open listening, be proactive when appropriate, and always interact with others with the intent of bringing out the best.

SUMMARY/CONCLUSIONS

I f you want to have a positive impact on others and the world, skillfully and consistently utilizing the practices discussed in this book with the intent to bring out the best in others, can lead to remarkable results. As an added benefit, when you are focused on bringing out the best in others, you almost always bring out the best in yourself.

In the 1970s, Alice Isen and Paul Levin conducted a study of helping behavior at two large shopping malls in San Francisco and Philadelphia.[30] This was back in the day when public telephones abounded, and you could make a local call for a dime. The experimenters took advantage of a simple behavior that almost everyone using public phones did: checking the coin return slot before dialing, during the call, or after hanging up.

The subjects were 24 adult women and 17 adult males who were shopping alone. Soon after an unsuspecting subject hung up and checked the coin return slot, a woman walking slightly ahead and to their side dropped a folder of papers in front of him/her. The variable of interest was if the phone caller would stop to help pick up the papers.

For half of the subjects, the experimenters had arranged for them to find a dime in the coin return slot; the other half found nothing. A large majority (88 percent) of subjects who had found the dime helped while only 4 percent of subjects who had found nothing helped.

In the same article, Isen and Levin reported another study which found that subjects who were given a cookie were much more likely to volunteer to help other experimental subjects than those who were not given a cookie. Conversely, subjects who were not given a cookie were more likely to volunteer to hinder experimental subjects than those given a cookie.

Two things strike us concerning the results of these and similar studies. One is how seemingly insignificant things (a dime or a cookie) can radically influence one's willingness to help another person.

The second implication of these studies is that situational factors (what has just happened) far outweigh personality characteristics of helping and being kind to others. While some people tend to be more generous and helpful compared to others, what happened to the person shortly before they had an opportunity to help or be kind to another was the major determinant of their helping behavior in the near future, at least in these studies.

In a 2014 report, Milena Tsvetkova and Michael W. Macy relate the following incident.

On a cold December morning in 2012, in the drive-through of the Tim Hortons in Winnipeg, Canada, a stranger generously picked up the tab for the coffee order of the next customer waiting in line. That person paid the bill of the next stranger in line, and so did the following 226 customers." Tsvetkova and Macy concluded that the results of their experiments "show that receiving and observing generosity can significantly increase the likelihood to be generous towards a stranger.[31]

___

What would happen in your family, community, country, and world if enough people adopted the goal of bringing out the best in themselves and others? After reviewing an enormous number of theories and volumes of data, Ken Wilber concluded that it takes about 10 percent of people in a society who are dedicated to a higher view to bring about change in the whole <u>society.</u> For instance, Wilber states it took about 10 percent of the population of the United States, who firmly believed in the immorality and injustice of the segregation and unfair treatment of minorities to bring about the civil rights movement.[32] Although many would agree that race is still an issue in America, it is clear that huge gains have been made in this area during 60 years.

Thus, what if 10 percent of the world's population developed a commitment to bring out the best in themselves and others with virtually every person they encountered or had some form of relationship with?

___

Let's look at this from a slightly different angle. You may be familiar with the notion of *six degrees of separation.* The idea is that each person on earth is connected to everyone else by six steps or fewer—everyone is at most *a friend of a friend of a friend of a friend of a friend of a friend.* Also, remember the contagiousness of feeling good and bringing out the best in yourself and others. Let's say you become committed to bringing out the best in people all the time as a guiding principle of your life. Today, you helped a friend bring out their best in a tough situation. If this friend also reaches out to a friend or stranger, and the process repeats four more times, the sixth person receiving compassionate help from a friend could be virtually any person on the planet. Doesn't this seem remarkable to you?

———————————

To extend this thought experiment, let's say that today you reach out to bring out the best in six people. Those six people do the same, and this process repeats eleven more times that day. If our math is correct, by the end of the day, there will have been over thirteen billion instances of people attempting to bring out the best in another person. Factoring in more than six billion duplications where the same person receives more than one attempt to bring out their best, almost every person on Earth will have gotten this nudge to bring out their best. (Since neither of us is an advanced mathematician, we are excited to hear from those who can either verify or debunk this idea.) And it all started with you reaching out in this way to six people. Then, what if you make a commitment to repeat this every day for the rest of your life?

———————————

Unfortunately, contagion effects (the spread of behaviors, beliefs, etc. through some type of contact) do not apply only to prosocial, generous, and helpful behaviors. For example, contagion is an accepted risk factor for suicide. It is also a likely factor in the increased disrespectful behavior and lack of civility in the United States and other places in the world. Research indicates that attitudes and emotions as well as actions can be influenced by contagion.

Back to the story of the two wolves that live inside us. Both the good and bad wolf live inside us. We don't have a choice; they are both there—it comes with being human. Whether you believe they are there due to evolution or Eve's big mistake, acknowledging they are both there is crucial.

The one you feed by your thoughts, feelings, and actions wins—becomes more powerful. But, like a conventional game or contest, the loser doesn't go away completely. There is always another game, and we need to keep working to stay on top of our game. As acknowledged at the beginning of this book, while you can more or less control the wolves inside yourself, you can also influence the wolves in others, primarily by how you treat them and also, more indirectly, by how you think and feel about them.

In western culture—particularly in the United States with which we are most familiar—the bad wolf seems to be taking over on many fronts. This should not discourage us but instead provide an impetus to fiercely feed the good wolf in ourselves as we treat everyone we meet in ways that will most likely bring out their best wolf. Encouraging the good wolf in others is synonymous with bringing out their best.

You might ask what if the other person is not treating you with respect or is doing things that bring you emotional harm? Recently a long-time friend and mentor, Jackie Garner, passed on a spiritual principle: *Our job is to love unconditionally; participation is optional.*

Loving unconditionally is an ideal to which we aspire but are likely to never achieve completely. Unconditional love means being as compassionate as possible toward everyone we meet, doing our best to see them as fellow humans, who like ourselves, want to be happy and avoid suffering.

However, this does not mean fully engaging with everyone, especially those who appear to want to take advantage or cause us harm. We are encouraging people to stretch their limits and to expand their thinking concerning in whom they want to bring out the best. However, this does not mean erasing all boundaries.

We were inspired to look at this from a somewhat different angle by the 2013 TED Talk by Mark Bowden.[33] Bowden points out that when we first see someone the primitive, unconscious, and automatic part of our mind (sometimes called the lizard brain) immediately decides, without conscious consultation, one of the following: 1) This person is someone from our tribe and would be safe and beneficial to affiliate with; 2) The person is a predator to be feared and either fought or run from; or 3) The person is not part of our tribe but not a predator and therefore of no interest to us.

Bowden believes that in modern society, most strangers are classified in the third category. This is to say that we quickly decide they are not meaningful and are best ignored. We automatically feel indifferent toward most strangers. He describes this as our most "authentic" way of feeling and acting—just going along with our primitive lizard brains.

We agree with Bowden that it takes deliberate conscious effort that utilizes the most recently evolved areas of our brain (the neocortex) and our highest mental perspective or worldview to override these automatic feelings, thoughts, and behaviors.

We disagree in calling our automatic feelings and actions the most authentic way of being. It may seem more natural for most of us to ignore strangers (and perhaps even people familiar to us) and just continue with whatever we are doing.

This might be the easiest thing to do and approaching them with the intent to bring out their best often takes us out of our comfort zone, at least at first.

Nevertheless, we believe that our most *authentic* actions come from using our entire brain, mind, soul, and Spirit. After all, it is our highly evolved (or created) neocortex that mostly differentiates us from other animals. Although our brains may contain a lizard-like element, we are clearly not lizards.

The idea that finding meaning in our lives is crucial in bringing satisfaction and happiness has been around for thousands of years but seemingly forgotten at times. How do we live a meaningful life? A quote by 19th Century British philosopher, John Stuart Mill, found in *The Power of Meaning: Finding Fulfillment in a World Obsessed with Happiness by* Emily Esfahani Smith, may say it best:

> Those only are happy who have their minds fixed on some object other than their own happiness; on the happiness of others, on the improvement of mankind, even on some art or pursuit followed not as a means, but as itself an ideal end. Aiming thus at something else, they find happiness by the way.[34]

We could also call this transcendence of the individual ego; first, it is a realization we are part of a much greater whole and then acting in line with this realization. It seems to us that *a commitment to bringing out the best in ourselves and others is a self-evident way to contribute to the well-being of ourselves and others as well as to the improvement of humankind in general.*

If you tend to go along with scientific findings, we are part of the seemingly infinite universe which has been brewing for around 13.8 billion years. And it took just a hair shy of those 13.8 billion years for life to develop self-reflective consciousness, at least on Earth. Self-reflective consciousness is our uniquely human ability to think about ourselves that includes thinking about our own thinking. Still, the odds of the universe developing in such a way that you can read and understand this book (or anything) is one in countless quadrillions.

You may believe in a God who designed and created the universe 13.8 billion or 6,000 years ago. You may believe the Divine or Spirit is a fundamental aspect of the entire universe, the creative spark that has driven the unique and increased complexity and self-organization of the exterior (physical) world as well the increased awareness, sensitivity, and awakening of the interior world—including your own consciousness. However, you may firmly hold that your present world is merely the result of random chance.

Whatever your beliefs are, hopefully, you can entertain the notion that a primary pattern guiding the history of the universe is *transcendence*. We are using the word transcend to mean to surpass, go beyond, and rise above. Without transcendence, our universe would be just a heap of atoms or whatever you believe the fundamental particles of the universe are. However, in our universe, atoms get together to transcend their individual functions by becoming molecules, molecules transcend to cell organelles, cell organelles to cells, cells to tissues, tissues to organs, organs to organ systems, and organ systems transcend to form the human body among countless other species.

And here we are. Don't you think it's time to use our self-reflective consciousness that has taken the universe billions of years to manifest to get beyond our own ego and journey further into inner transcendence? Working toward inner transcendence through contemplative prayer, meditation, and other methods are helpful and often necessary for transcending to more inclusive worldviews.

However, using our expanded worldviews to go beyond our ego's needs and motives with concrete actions is also critically needed in our physical world. We believe that focusing on *bringing out the best in others* is a splendid way to transcend—both in interior and exterior dimensions. *It is ultimately up to each of us, as individuals, to commit to bringing out the best in ourselves and others—or not.*

You get to decide.

You have three choices whenever the opportunity to interact with another person arises.

1. Ignore them
2. Do what is likely to bring out their worst
3. Do what is likely to bring out their best

The Invitation

We invite you to commit to bring out the best in yourself and others. We believe that a worthy purpose or continuing goal in any relationship is to bring out the best in yourselves and each other.

ABOUT THE AUTHORS

R ick and Sheila's careers have focused on working with individuals and families to help them better communicate, understand, and cooperate with each other.

After working as a psychologist for the State of Arizona, Rick pursued private practice, specializing in ADHD and behavioral and learning problems for most of his career. He engaged in a solo practice from 2005 through 2016.

Sheila has worked with people of all ages in school systems, mental health agencies, and the business world. She has provided teaching, training, counseling, and inspiration in these settings.

After raising their two daughters, Amy and Sara, in the

Midwest, they currently reside with their cat on a mountainside above a small town in Panama.

They enjoy art, music, gardening, raising butterflies, reading mystery novels, learning Spanish, traveling, and writing about bringing out the best. They invite you to join their adventures at volweider.com.

If you have not already done so, be sure to get your **free** copy of Rick and Amy's *Quick Guide to Mindfulness*, which now contains four guided meditations, in both audio and transcript forms. This guide expands upon material presented in this book.

Download Your Free Guided Mindfulness Meditations and Book Here: https://forms.aweber.com/form/99/2138863799.htm

PLEASE HELP US

Reviews help us improve our writing and help reach potential readers. We would much appreciate your leaving an honest review at Amazon.com.

Thanks so much!

Rick and Sheila Volweider

NOTES

1   These quotes are from a 2012 Interview with Dweck we found at https://en.wikipedia.org/wiki/Carol_Dweck.

2   Warneken, F. (2013). The development of altruistic behavior: Helping in children and chimpanzees. Social Research, 80(2), 431-442. Retrieved from http://nrs.harvard.edu/urn-3:HUL.InstRepos:12285465.

3   In our adaption of the shadow process, we have focused on situations where we feel angry, hostile, irritated, or repelled by another person. In Integral Life Practice. Wilber, et al., expand situations related to shadow work. We recommend pages 41 to 66 for a more complete introduction to shadow work and believe their entire book would be well worth reading.

4   Axness, M. (2012) Parenting for Peace: Raising the Next Generatio of Peacemakers. Boulder, CO: Sentient Publications. P. 98.

5   Krznaric, R. Six habits of highly empathic people. Retrieved December 3,2017 from https://greatergood.berkeley.edu/article/item/six_habits_of_highly_empathic_people1.

6   Ibid. Paragraph 21

7   Ibid. Paragraph 24.

8   We found this quote in Watkins A., & Wilber, K. (2015). Wicked and Wise: How to Solve the World's Toughest Problems. Kent, Great Britain: Urbane Publication, Kindle Edition. Loc 2650.

9   Pollan, M. (2009) Food rules: An eater's manual. New York: Penfuin Books. Kindle version.

10   Quote is from Food Rules by M. Pollan. Kindle version, Introduction, paragraph 7.

11   These statistics were retrieved from the following internet sources:
<u>During that year 19,885 Americans died of heroin and:</u> Accessed on 8/1/2017 from http://www.washingtontimes.com/news/2016/dec/13/the-mounting-death-toll-from-illicit-drugs/
<u>20 were killed by Islamic terrorists</u>: Accessed on 8/1/2017 from http://www.snopes.com/toddlers-killed-americans-terrorists/
<u>21 were shot dead by toddlers</u>: Accessed on 8/1/2017 from http://www.snopes.com/toddlers-killed-americans-terrorists/
<u>15,696 people were murdered</u>: Accessed on 8/1/2017 from https://www.nytimes.com/2016/09/27/us/murder-crime-fbi.html
<u>38,300 were killed in car accidents</u>: Accessed on 8/1/2017 from http://www.newsweek.com/2015-brought-biggest-us-traffic-death-increase-50-years-427759
<u>Compare that with 536,224 deaths by heart disease</u>: Accessed 8/1/2017 from http://news.heart.org/u-s-death-rate-rises-slightly-in-2015-as-heart-disease-deaths-level-off/
<u>and 589,430 deaths due to cancer</u>: American Cancer So-

ciety, Cancer Facts & Figures 2015._Accessed on 8/1/2017 from https://www.cancer.org/research/cancer-facts-statistics/all-cancer-facts-figures/cancer-facts-figures-2015.html

12   Constine, J. (2016). How Facebook News Feed Works. Accessed 8/1/2017 from https://techcrunch.com/2016/09/06/ultimate-guide-to-the-news-feed/#

13   Back in 2012, I (Rick) spent many hours watching political coverage. I found it entertaining to watch commentators on FOX News and then MSNBC report on the same video clip. Not only were their conclusions extremely different, it often sounded like they were describing two completely different video clips. And they were both pretty convincing!

14   Accessed 11-22-2018 from https://en.wikiquote.org/wiki/Werner_Heisenberg

15   McConaughey, Matthew (May 27, 2018). "This Is Why You're Not Happy" You Tube Video. Accessed from https://www.youtube.com/watch?v=p0p1fjLPjYQ

16   Rosenthal, Robert (1994). Interpersonal Expectancy Effects: A 30-Year Perspective. Current Directions in Psychological Science. Sage Journals. P. 176. Accessed from https://journals.sagepub.com/doi/10.1111/1467-8721.ep10770698

17   Ibid. P. 176.

18   You can view a summary of the Yale baby studies at https://www.youtube.com/watch?v=FRvVFW85IcU&spfreload=10.

19 Quote from Stephen Mitchell's translation of the Bhagavad Gita, Verses 2.47 and 2.50. Mitchell, S. (2000). Bhagavad Gita: A New Translation. New York: Harmony Books. Kindle version.

20 The article, by Cheryl Posey, which we retrieved 5/1/2017 appears to no longer exists at https://www.diahannboock.com/articles/Tone-Voice. You can find more about Ms. Posey at her Linkedin page at https://www.linkedin.com/in/cherylposey/.

21 Mann, D. (2017) Connect with anyone: How to be instantly likable, irresistibly charming, and quickly connect with people on a deep level. (Kindle version).

22 Institute of Judicial Studies (2013). Albert Meridian Communication Studies. Accessed 11-4-2018 from http://www.iojt-dc2013.org/~/media/Microsites/Files/IOJT/11042013-Albert-Mehrabian-Communication-Studies.ashx

23 Mann, D. (2017) Connect with anyone: How to be instantly likable, irresistibly charming, and quickly connect with people on a deep level. (Kindle version) Retrieved from amazon.com. p. 24.

24 Ibid. p. 25.

25 Berman, E. & Berman, D. (2012). People Skills at Work. Boca Raton, FL: CRC Press.

26 Zabelina, D. L. and Robinson, M. D. (2010). Child's

play: Facilitating the originality of creative output by a priming manipulation. Psychology of Aesthetics, Creativity, and the Arts., 4(1), 57–65.

27   Dalai Lama, Tutu, D., & Abrams, D. (2016). The Book of Joy: Lasting Happiness in a Changing World. New York USA: Penguin-Random House. Kindle version. p. 216.

28   Ibid. p. 216.

29   Cousins, N (1979). Anatomy of an illness as perceived by the patient: Reflections on healing and regeneration. Originally Published 1979. Kindle Edition published by Open Road Integrated Media, New York. (Kindle version). Accessed from amazon.com

30   Isen, A. M. & Levin, P. F. (1972). The effect of feeling good On helping: Cookies and kindness. Journal of Personality and Social Psychology, 21(3), 384-388.

31   Tsvetkova, Milena and Macy, Michael W. (2014). The Social Contagion of Generosity. PLoS One. 9(2): e87275. Retrieved 8-27-2018 from https://www.ncbi.nlm.nih.gov/pmc/articles/PMC3923723/

32   Wilber, Ken (date not given) Trump And A Post-Truth World: An Evolutionary Self-correction. Integral Life. p. 72. Accessed from http://www.integrallife.com/.

33   The Importance of Being Inauthentic. TED Talk by Mark Bowden. September 2013. Retrieved 1-6-2018 from https://www.youtube.com/watch?v=1zpf8H_Dd40.

34 Smith, E. (2017). The Power of Meaning: Finding Fulfillment in a World Obsessed with Happiness. New York: Broadway Books. P. 16. Kindle version.

Made in the USA
San Bernardino, CA
26 February 2020